D'sember, 1861, Wed. 25

Christmiss Day. Don't go till a shootin' match, nor
a dance, nor a join, nor don't play pins; bekase ye
see it's wrong t' do them things the day. Jist take
my advice, stay at home an' mind yer book; or
mebby go t' church, if that's where ye belong to;
an' hes nothing betther t' do.

Billy McCart, *Poor Rabbin's Ollminick for the Town
O'Bilfawst*, 1861

THE SECOND IRISH CHRISTMAS BOOK

Edited by
John Killen

THE
BLACKSTAFF
PRESS

BELFAST AND WOLFEBORO, NEW HAMPSHIRE

First published in 1986 by
The Blackstaff Press
3 Galway Park, Dundonald, Belfast BT16 0AN, Northern Ireland
and
27 South Main Street, Wolfeboro, New Hampshire 03894 USA
with the assistance of
The Arts Council of Northern Ireland

Printed in Northern Ireland by
The Universities Press Limited

British Library Cataloguing in Publication Data
The Second Irish Christmas Book.
1. Christmas — Literary collections   2. English
literature — Irish authors
I. Killen, John, 1954–
820.8′033   PR8836.5.C4

Library of Congress Cataloging-in-Publication Data
The Second Irish Christmas Book.
Includes index.
1. Christmas — Literary collections.   2. English
literature — Irish authors.   3. Ireland — Literary
collections.   4. Christmas — Ireland.   I. Killen, John,
1954–   II. Title: Irish Christmas Book.
PR8836.5.C48S4   1986   820′.8′033   86–17620
ISBN 0 85640 371 7

CONTENTS

FOREWORD

Christmas in Ireland! The very words conjure up a picture of the happiness, piety and celebrations of a small, mainly rural population inhabiting a tiny island off the European landmass – an island where traditional values are preserved in a truer and more holy form than elsewhere in this wicked world.

The reality, however, as depicted by some of Ireland's leading writers, is less straightforward than the stereotype, and is infinitely more varied. The festivities, pieties and fun-seeking of a great but venal people have produced a literary legacy rich in incident and anecdote. True religious piety is contrasted with the increasing commercialisation of Christmas; sumptuous living in the big house with the most meagre fare enjoyed by the peasants of the west of Ireland; urban festivities with rural.

Humour abounds: the unfettered humour of a vital people, often faced with adversity, sometimes with tragedy. In the muddy carnage of Flanders a young Irish soldier is able to create a night of feasting and carousing; while, in an H-block of the Maze Prison an internee, with the connivance of his guards, can celebrate an uproarious and inebriate Christmas. Pathos, that sentiment so close to the heart of the Irish (especially when in drink), is to be found here: the pathos of the Irishman in London on Christmas Eve, vainly seeking to recreate a semblance of his native land in the saloon bar of a Highbury pub.

Great events contrast with the commonplace to give us a truer picture of Christmas in Ireland, as it has been celebrated by generations of Irishmen and women, and by generations of exiles and of fleeting visitors. Handel in Dublin, Peig Sayers in Dingle, a Brian Moore character in Belfast and an unknown exile in London all have a story to tell and all add to our understanding and enjoyment.

When I began selecting material for the first *Irish Christmas Book* in 1985 I quickly realised that the sheer quantity and quality of the 'eligible' writing would prove to be my greatest problem. There was simply too much for one volume – and the only solution was to publish a second. So I'm now pleased to offer, like the ingredients of a Christmas pudding, another collection of varied and variegated stories and poems, blending together to produce a tempting and, at times, surprising literary *mélange* for our entertainment and enlightment.

John Killen, 1986

A CLONEY CAROL

D.M. Large

If it was to Cloney
That they chanced to come
When the roads were stony
And the birds were dumb;
Just a tired man, striding
By a small grey ass,
And a woman riding,
Would we let them pass?

If they craved for shelter
Would we with a 'No',
Send them through the welter
Of the drifting snow?
Would the house be crowded
Where the fire was bright,
Must they still go, shrouded
In the mists of night?

Must they seek a stable
In some yard outside;
Would the straw be able
Cobbles hard to hide?
Would we wonder only
Who are they at all?
Must the woman, lonely
Dress the baby small?

If it was tomorrow
That they came our way
Would we give them sorrow
With the words we'd say?
If it was to Cloney
That they chanced to come,
When the roads are stony
And the birds are dumb.

The Cloney Carol, 1934

HAPPY CHRISTMAS!

David Armstrong with Hilary Saunders

It was Christmas Day 1983. I was standing at the back of the church greeting families as they arrived for the service, admiring the toys that the children had brought to show me (I had said that I would be glad to see any Christmas presents except livestock!), and chatting to members of the choir. The whole place had a festive atmosphere, with a Christmas tree and crib and lovely decorations. Everyone seemed happy and relaxed and once again I was glad to have initiated this Christmas Day service two years previously.

Ten minutes before the service was due to begin, Aubrey Douglas, a longstanding elder, came up to me as I was talking to two small children. He smiled at me, 'One of your friends is in the vestibule by the front door,' he said. 'Which friend?' I asked. 'Go and see!' he said with a smile. I went down to the front door of the church where I could see old Willie Thompson, our senior elder, shaking hands with someone. As I got closer I realised that the man he was greeting was Father Kevin Mullan. I was very surprised to see him in my church, but at the same time very pleased.

'David, I have just popped across the road to ask if you would relay a message from me to your congregation; I want to say Happy Christmas and trust that the blessing of Our Lord be upon them over the Christmas period. I have come to say to you that my people across the road wish your people a Happy Christmas!' I looked him straight in the eye: 'Well,

Kevin, our service is just about to start. Before we begin I'll get people's attention and you can wish them Happy Christmas yourself.' He hestitated, 'Well if you're sure you don't mind.' I think he was rather taken aback, but he followed me into the church.

There was a happy buzz of noise; people greeting one another, children laughing and talking. Today was a festival occasion and we were going to have a special celebration this morning, the baptism of a new-born baby. As I looked over the congregation I could see the baby and his parents and I thought what a lovely visual aid they were to remind us of the birth of Jesus and what his life on earth meant. It seemed very appropriate that Father Mullan should be here too.

I clapped my hands, calling for people's attention: 'Please settle down now and listen to me! The clergyman from across the road has just popped in and he's going to wish you a Happy Christmas!' That is exactly what he did. He asked the people to accept his best wishes for Christmas from him and from his congregation across the road. I thought my people would receive him politely, it was Christmas after all, but I was taken by surprise at the spontaneous applause that greeted his message. As Father Mullan made his way down the aisle to the door people reached over to greet him and shake his hand. It was a very moving sight for me.

At the end of our service I shook hands with everyone as they left, and duly admired all the new toys. Everyone seemed very happy and no one made any objection to Father Mullan's visit. I suppose I had wondered if some people would be angry, but basically the man had only said 'Happy Christmas!' After everyone had left I stood outside watching the cars drive away. I could hear singing coming from the Roman Catholic church, and remembering that their service had started fifteen minutes after ours, I guessed that this was the sound of their closing hymn.

I walked across the road and through the glass doors into the church. The hymn was just finishing, and I realised that Father Kevin could see me standing there. As people moved around to pick up their belongings Father Kevin clapped his hands and asked everyone to sit down. 'Although the service is over I'd ask you to wait for a moment, because David Armstrong, the Presbyterian minister from across the road, is here and I think he wants to pass on his greetings to you.'

I felt a little bit conspicuous as I walked to the front, well aware that everyone was watching me. I turned and wished them all a Happy Christmas, asking for peace and understanding in our community, and praying for the love of Christ in the New Year. 'I want to wish you God's richest blessing at Christmas time, the time when the Prince of Peace came into our world.' As I finished speaking there was a very strong and loud burst of spontaneous applause and people gathered round me wanting to greet me. By the time I got home for lunch my hand was aching from being shaken so many times! I told June where I had been and we talked about Kevin Mullan's visit to our church. We agreed that it was indeed a very happy Christmas!

Over the next few days I received some lovely letters from members of the Catholic church. I remember one in particular from a lady in her late seventies, who said she had spent many Christmases in Limavady but this one had been the happiest she had ever experienced because the Presbyterian minister from across the road had come in to wish her the blessing of Christ. I was very moved as I read her letter, realising that what had after all been a very simple action had meant so much to her.

As I took up my normal visiting patterns again after Christmas I went to see members of my congregation both in hospital and at home. Everyone greeted me warmly, and I didn't encounter any anger or hostility about Father Mullan's visit. I was glad to see that my congregation had such a healthy attitude, and began to feel that the love of Jesus was beginning to break through some of the barriers and prejudices in the community.

In the middle of January Aubrey Douglas had a heart attack and was seriously ill in hospital. He had another two attacks in hospital and June and I were very worried about him. I tried to spend as much time as possible praying by his bedside, supporting his wife, daughter and brother Mervyn.

By now Ivan Bryne had stepped down from being session clerk and his place had been taken by Henry Harbinson, a well-respected farmer. Henry was a committed Christian and a great prayer warrior and I had grown close to him when his only daughter had been seriously injured in a car accident. We had spent many anxious hours together praying for her full recovery and had been thrilled to see how God answered our prayers. Out of that, Henry and I had developed a good relationship and I was delighted to have him as session clerk.

When he contacted me at the end of January to say that he had been asked to call a meeting of the session, I asked what it was to be about. It had been a rule at Carrickfergus that whenever someone wanted to raise an issue at a session meeting they would tell the person concerned in advance, so that they would have time to find out all the relevant details about the matter. I thought this was a fair rule and had tried to introduce it when I came to Limavady. So when I asked Henry what the meeting was going to be about and he didn't know the answer, I was rather surprised. All he could tell me was that Connolly George had asked him to call the meeting and he was not sure what it was about.

Ten days before the meeting I met Connolly George and his wife in the church grounds when I was on my way home for lunch. This was my opportunity to ask him about the session meeting and find out what he wanted us to discuss. 'Connolly, I believe you have called this session meeting and I wonder if you could tell me what it's going to be about?' I asked. 'You will find out when you get there,' he replied enigmatically. 'Can't you tell me now?' I asked. 'Do you mean to say you don't know?' There was a hint of disbelief in his voice. 'I honestly don't know; please do tell me.' 'Well,' he said, 'it's all about the priest being in the church.' 'That was on Christmas Day! What's the problem now?' 'You're not to do things like that,' he said.

A Road Too Wide, 1985

CHRISTMAS

STAY THEE AWHILE, UPSPRINGING HEART,
THOU WILD AND FROWARD THING.
HERE HOMING YEARS HAVE SET APART
GIFTS PAST IMAGINING.
HERE THOU SHALL PLUME FOR STRONGER FLIGHT,
LEARN TRUER SONGS TO SING.
MEMORY SHALL GIVE THEE CLEARER SIGHT,
LOVE DEARER CHERISHING.
SUSAN L. MITCHELL.

5

THE CHRISTMAS MUMMERS

Patrick Kavanagh

Apology

This is the stuff of which I was made,
The crude loud homespun bagging at the knees,
The primitive but not simple barbarities,
The casual labourer with an unskilful spade.
Unsimple ignorance was our only trade;
Our minds untrained to tensions would not seize
The string and stretch it till sincerity's
Tune to the pain-nobled end was played.
We shouted on mountains, but no god gathered
The wise sayings and the extraordinarily pure notes;
All went for nothing, a whole nation blathered
Without art, which is Character's city name.
And that is the story, the reason for the trailing coats;
The unmannerly bravado is the bluff of shame.

The Roomer

Room, room my gallant boys and give us room to rhyme,
We'll show you some activity coming on this Christmastime;
We act the rich, we act the poor, the simple and the critical,
We act the scenes that lie behind the public and political
We bring you noble statesmen and poets loused with song
And actors who make stacks of money making fun,
And if you don't believe me and give in to what I say
I'll call in Seamus O'Donavan and he'll soon clear the way.

Seamus O'Donavan

Here comes I Seamus O'Donavan – against the British menace
I fought when I was younger in the War of Independence;
Encouraged the national language, too old myself to learn it –
And if I got a pension who says I didn't earn it?
In days when 'The Emergency' was no poor cow in labour
But war most awful threatening the world and our neighbour
I took my musket down and joined young men who were no moochers
But soldiering nobly for the land into congenial futures;
My face as you can see is clear-marked old ITA,
An Irish face, good-natured, Catholic, liberal and gay
My hair is turning whitish (though in youth severely mauled,
Oddly, no man who ever fought for Ireland goes quite bald).
For the good name of my country I am most insanely zealous
And of comrades who got richer I am not the least bit jealous
And if you don't believe me and give in to what I say
I'll call in a Successful Statesman and he'll soon clear the way.

Successful Statesman

Here comes I a Successful Statesman, from the people I am sprung
My father a National Teacher learned in Gaelic rune and song;
My mother was of ancient stock and early taught to me
The fear of God and daily toil and common poverty.
By the worthy Christian Brothers my character was shaped
And we prayed for Mother Erin when by Saxons she was raped;
I played my part in the struggle – played football for my country
And won an All-Ireland medal when I was barely twenty.
And I never deserted poetry – God be good to poor Owen Roe!
And the thousand Kerry poets who were slaughtered by the foe.
And if you don't believe me and give in to what I say
I'll call in Sean Óg O'Gum and he'll soon clear the way.

Sean Óg O'Gum
Here comes I Sean Óg O'Gum, seven pounds have I
Retainer from the Government for writing poetry:
I write about tinker tribes and porter-drinking men
Who shoulder-shove their minds into the handle of my pen.
The clans are scything song again on rebel-ripened hills
And reason screams for mercy at the stratching of our quills.
We know a hundred thousand ways for saying 'Drink your liquor'
When we toss the coin of language ne'er a ha'penny comes a sticker.
No truck have we with pagans or the foreign-backside licker.
I set my boat's proud prow to sea and hoist my ballad sails
And chant on decks of destiny for the all-too-silent Gaels
And if you don't believe me and give in to what I say
I'll call in a Famous Actor and he'll soon clear the way.

Famous Actor
Here comes I, a Famous Actor of films stage and radio,
I was born the son of a peasant in the county of Mayo;
I am the man they call on to speak the verse of Sean
And other Gaelic poets, and lately I have done
A lot of work in English that's well out of the groove –
The popular taste in culture we are aiming to improve;
And last week when adjudicating at a Drama Festival,
I found that Irish audiences liked Eliot best of all.
I've escaped the grind of daily toil and cabins dirty, smelly
And I'm married to the daughter of Senator O'Kelly,
And if you don't believe me and give in to what I say
I'll call in Senator O'Kelly and he'll soon clear the way.

Senator O'Kelly
Here comes I Senator O'Kelly a simple businessman,
I make no claims to culture though I do the best I can
To foster our great artists and though business presses so
I go to exhibitions and I spend a lot of dough.
And one thing most I do regret, a thing to me most shocking
And that is certain critics who are far too fond of knocking
The men who make their country known throughout the artistic sphere
Earning dollars with the pictures at which these fellows sneer.
As a common or garden businessman this attitude I deplore
But I thank God for our vigilant Press which shuts on them its door.
And if you don't believe me and give in to what I say
I'll call in a Leading Editor and he'll soon clear the way.

Leading Editor

Here comes I a Leading Editor who knows the Irish dream,
I'm open to every idea that fits in with the regime:
The Liberal Opposition who complain of bishops' mitres
And the rising cost of turnips and the censorship on writers.
The Press is free, the radio gives them a free debate,
New Statesmanism is essential to every well-run state.
These are not Lilliputian cranks as destructive critics scream
They are the Official Liberal Opposition and part of the regime.
And if you don't believe me and give in to what I say
Go to the bogs or Birmingham or Mountjoy right away.

The Hitler war was known officially in Southern Ireland as 'The Emergency'.

Owen Roe. Owen Roe Sullivan was in the front rank of the ten thousand Irish poets of his day. The standing army of Irish poets seldom falls below this figure.

Football prowess in Ireland, as in Hungary today, has always been a path to political success.

Contrived, manufactured verse with its necessary lack of any passionate impulse or belief is what passed for poetry among the Gaels. Phrase-making. The poet was a romantically wild man who was seldom sober, was a devil for the women. Dylan Thomas brought this bogusity to the English who thought it new and wonderful.

New Statesmanism. The *New Statesman* is the name of an English radical weekly.

Mountjoy is the principal Dublin jail.

Working on the turf bogs in Ireland is equivalent to salt-mining in Siberia.

The surplus Irish population who cannot get into the BBC work in Birmingham where they are to be seen high up in the sky painting gasometers.

The Complete Poems of Patrick Kavanagh, 1964

CHRISTMAS IN ENGLAND

George Bernard Shaw

These are not busy times for musical critics. In London everything serves as an excuse for having no music, from the death of a Royal personage to Christmas, just as in school everything serves as an excuse for a holiday. I have been in the country, in an old-English manorhouse, where we all agreed to try and forget the festive season. We were not altogether successful. On the very first evening we were invaded by 'the mummers,' who were not in the least like the husbands of Mr George Moore's Mummer's Wife. They were laborers, overgrown with strips of colored paper as a rock is overgrown with seaweed; and they went through an operatic performance which I did not quite follow, as they were quite equal to professional opera singers in point of unintelligibility, and, being simple country folk, were so unversed in the etiquette of first nights that they neglected to provide me with a libretto.

I gathered that one of them was King Alfred, and another St George. A third, equipped with a stale tall hat, was announced as 'the doctor'. He drew a tooth from the prima donna, whom I did not succeed in identifying; revived the other characters when they were slain in single combat; and sang a ballad expressive of his aspiration to live and die 'a varmer's b'woy'. This he delivered with such a concentrated lack of conviction that I at once concluded that he actually was a farmer's boy;

10

and my subsequent inquiries as to the rate of wages in the district confirmed my surmise.

We of the audience had to assume the character of good old English gentlemen and ladies keeping up a seasonable custom; and it would be difficult to say whether we or the performers were the most put out of countenance. I have seldom been so disconcerted; and my host, though he kept it up amazingly, confessed to sharing my feelings; whilst the eagerness of the artists to escape from our presence when their performance was concluded and suitably acknowledged, testified to the total failure of our efforts to make them feel at home. We were perfectly friendly at heart, and would have been delighted to sit round the fire with them and talk; but the conventions of the season forbade it. Since we had to be mock-baronial, they had to be mock-servile; and so we made an uneasy company of Christmas humbugs, and had nothing to cheer us except the consciousness of heartily forgiving one another and being forgiven.

On Christmas Eve there was more music, performed by the schoolchildren, the carol-singers, and finally by an orchestra consisting of a violin, a tambourine, a toy instrument with a compass of one wrong note, which it played steadily on the second and third beats in the bar, and anything else that would make a noise *ripieno, ad lib*. The singers sang traditional – i.e. inaccurate – versions of old airs and modern music-hall songs, the latter strangely modified by transmission from mouth to ear along the whole length of the Thames.

Music in London 1890–94, 1932

A CHAT ABOUT MONEY

Patrick Campbell

'The words of the wise are as goads, and as nails fastened by the masters of assemblies, which are given from one shepherd.'

I didn't know what it meant, but it was the Lord all right. He was certainly the master of the assembly that was gathered every Christmas Day around the remnants of the lunch table. The assembly consisted of my brother and myself, and it was convened by the Lord in his usual diffident and conspiratorial fashion.

Before lunch he'd say to me, very privately, something like, 'We'd better have a bit of a chat about money, after lunch. If you could get Michael to stay. . .'

Like myself, Michael would not have missed these occasions for anything.

The subject under review was the avoidance of death duties, and the imperative need for the Lord to hand over to Michael and myself the monies held in the Glenavy Trust. The Lord always called them 'the monies', probably with the intention of giving them the sacrosanct and untouchable quality of the Crown Jewels.

He would begin, every Christmas Day, by reviewing the history of the Trust, Michael and I having another brandy and the Lord pouring himself a second bottle of stout.

The opening theme was always the hopeless situation that had been created by the Old Lord's will. So far as Michael and I could make out, the Old Lord, in the last years of his life, had lost a great deal of money on the Stock Exchange, but had taken no account of this in his will. In fact, he hadn't left sufficient 'monies' to cover his numerous bequests.

At this point Michael would sometimes say, in a carefully casual manner, 'How much did he leave?' – and the Lord would reply that he'd come to that in a moment.

The next and equally apalling facet of the situation was the clause in the Old Lord's will that said that 'the monies' in the Trust should go to the holder of the title of Lord Glenavy.

'This,' said the Lord, with evident satisfaction, 'has given Archie and myself some fearful headaches. Legally, you see, Paddy, I can't give it to you until you're Lord Glenavy and –' the bent forefinger would come out, gently stabbing the air – 'you won't be Lord Glenavy until I've passed on.'

He would look at both of us intently, to see if we had any glimmering of understanding of this abstruse and complex point.

Michael and I would nod, our brows furrowed in concentration, trying not to meet one another's eye.

'But, you see,' the Lord would go on, 'if I – pass – on before – doing something about it, you and Michael are going to be absolutely bankrupted by the appalling death duties.'

'They'd be pretty big?' I'd suggest.

'Yes. So Archie and I have been working night and day to try to find some way out of the mess. I must say, Archie's been marvellous, but it's killing him. He's not looking at all well. At this rate he'll go before I do and then we'll all be finally ruined.'

At this point Michael and I knew we would be safe in sitting back and abandoning for another year all hope of discovering anything about our financial prospects. The Lord had worked himself into his favourite morass, buried so deeply in a pit of troubles that he could see no gleam of hope anywhere, and determined to make it impossible for either of us to do anything else except join him.

For the next half hour he would give us a review of the prohibitive cost of running the house. 'Beattie's got to have a car and the cook's wages have gone up and the fence has fallen down in the lower field. . .' From these domestic burdens he would pass to more serious matters. They were always centred around his certainty that in the next couple of months he would be stripped of all his directorships. 'They don't like Protestants, you see, and they can't wait to get me out.' In this welter of approaching disaster, however, he was prepared to give us one piece of good news. 'I suppose the Bank would probably keep me on, as I'm the only person that knows anything about it.' But it was instantly neutralised by the threat of a greater catastrophe than any we'd been faced with yet – the threat not merely of personal bankruptcy, but of bankruptcy on a national scale.

'This present Government,' the Lord would say, savouring every word, 'simply hasn't got the faintest idea what it's doing. Lemass is all right but the rest of them couldn't run a village shop in – in Ballyslumgullion. The trade figures are appalling. They're recklessly importing every kind of trivial foreign luxury at prohibitive cost and all they can do in exchange is send a few flea-bitten cows to England. Within the next couple of months you'll see the biggest economic crash here since the American Depression and then God knows what will become of Beattie –'

Michael and I always knew that the prospect of Beattie scrubbing floors in abject penury was an indication that the Lord was feeling better and that the talk had almost come to an end. This would be confirmed when he'd suddenly say, 'Anyway, you and Michael don't have to worry. There's plenty of money there.'

In some curious way this reassurance seemed to be the logical outcome of all that had gone before. Then the Lord would say, reaching for the brandy, 'Give me a swash of that stuff there.' He'd pour himself half a glassful, throw it straight down, and say, 'I suppose we'd better try a bit of croquet before the rain.'

Another assembly had come to an end, leaving Michael and myself as totally ignorant of the financial situation and of what, if anything, was going to be done about it, as before.

My Life and Easy Times, 1967

CHRISTMAS IN IRELAND

Lady Mabel Annesley

In Ireland, Christmas was the event of the year. I can still see the lighted, holly-decked kitchen, with its high beamed roof like a church. Joints of meat on spits turned in front of an immense open fire. Rows of coppers shone like setting suns on the dressers. Busy maids flew about the sanded stone floors. They were presided over by the cook in a beribboned conical cap, beneath which a fat face descended in double chins. She was bolstered in print and linen, stiff and starched: a pyramid of flesh. But in her profession she was a consummate artist.

As the Sight is Bent, 1964

THE GOOSE

Michael Longley

Remember the white goose in my arms,
A present still. I plucked the long
Flight-feathers, down from the breast,
Finest fuzz from underneath the wings.

I thought of you through the operation
And covered the unmolested head,
The pink eyes that had persisted in
An expression of disappointment.

It was right to hesitate before
I punctured the skin, made incisions
And broached with my reluctant fingers
The chill of its intestines, because

Surviving there, lodged in its tract,
Nudging the bruise of the orifice
Was the last egg. I delivered it
Like clean bone, a seamless cranium.

Much else followed which, for your sake,
I bundled away, burned on the fire
With the head, the feet, the perfect wings.
The goose was ready for the oven.

I would boil the egg for your breakfast,
Conserve for weeks the delicate fats
As in the old days. In the meantime
We dismantled it, limb by limb.

Poems 1963–1983, 1985

CHRISTMAS EVE IN DINGLE

Peig Sayers

Christmas Eve fell on a Tuesday and everyone was busy preparing for it. Seáinín came in the door carrying a bundle of ivy and holly.

'Give me a hand, Margaret,' he said, 'till I fasten this to the window.'

'I know nothing about it,' I said, 'because I never saw it done.'

'You'll see it now, girl, and when it'll be fixed up it will be simply beautiful.'

Anna and Eibhlín were busy making paper flowers of every colour; according as they had a flower finished Seáinín would tuck it in among the ivy.

'Bring me the candle now,' he told me.

I got a great red candle and a candlestick; this he set on the window-sill.

'Make the tea, you,' he told me, 'while I'm fixing up the rest of it.'

I hung the kettle over the fire and while I was waiting for it to boil I fixed the table in the middle of the kitchen. Seáinín told me to get a blue candle, to light it and place it on the table. When I had it lighting I laid the table with delf for the tea. Then Nell got up, and bringing with her three kinds of bread, she sliced it on a bread board. There was plenty jam and butter on the table too and when all the lights were lighting and the kitchen was decorated I thought that I was in the Kingdom of Heaven because I had never before seen such a lovely sight. Nell poured out the tea and everyone sat down to the table; they were all pleasant and cheerful, especially Nell. Every single move her family made filled her with joy.

I was watching them very closely as I drank my tea. Thoughts ran into my mind: I was thinking of my poor mother at that time. I knew the kind of a night she had, a near-sighted, lonely, unfortunate woman without light or joy for I was the one comfort she had in this life. I was far away from her now and I couldn't raise her spirits nor offer her a scrap of happiness.

'The way of the world is strange,' I told myself. 'Look at Nell and the comfort she draws from her family and there are other poor mothers who never get the slightest scrap of satisfaction out of life.'

In spite of all the pleasure around me tears came to my eyes. Seáinín noticed me. 'Margaret is lonesome,' he said.

He came over to me from the other side of the table and began to give me soft talk so as to take my mind off my loneliness.

'Seáinín,' I told him, 'I'm not a bit lonely in the way you imagine, but I was thinking of my mother. Go back and drink your tea.' Then I began eating just like he was.

When we had the supper eaten and all the things were set aside Séamas came in with a bottle of wine and a glass in his hand. 'Would ye like punch?' he asked us.

'We would, Daddy,' the children said. 'This is Christmas Eve!'

'I don't care for wine at all, darlin',' Nan said. 'I prefer a little drop of whiskey.'

Back he went and then returned with a jugful of whiskey.

'Here, take your pick of them!' he said.

Nell made a small drop of wine-negus that was suitable for the family and she gave me a fair jorum of it too.

'Won't you have a drop yourself, Missus?' I asked her.

'I won't, child,' she said. 'I never let a spoonful of drink pass my lips nor would I give it to these children but as little but for respect for the night that's there.'

'Would you be afraid you'd get drunk?' I asked, for curiosity was picking me.

'Not that, child, but it has always been said: "Taste the food and you'll get fond of it." I don't think there was ever a person who was sipping and tipping at drink but got a mind for it in the latter end.'

Séamaisín and Eibhlín were over at the window-sill examining the small lovely pictures that Seáinín had placed here and there. Eibhlín took one of them in her hand and went over where Nan was.

'Nan,' she said, 'look at the nice little lamb with his feet tied.'

'Aye,' said Nan, 'that's the Blessed Infant whom we all adore tonight.'

'Why does He take the shape of a lamb?' the child wanted to know.

'Sit down there quietly,' Nan said, 'and I'll tell you.' They all sat down.

'At that time a king of high rank called Herod ruled the district where Mary and the Infant were living. He heard about the child Jesus and made up his mind to put to death every male child under the age of three months. He ordered his bodyguard and his soldiers to guard the great city of Bethlehem and not to allow anyone in or out without first finding out all about their business. Immediately the order was received, sentries and guards were posted in every street, at every street corner and on every road and highway. Mary had a close friend called Bríghde and when *she* heard the news she went to Mary who, when she saw her coming, gave her a warm welcome. "Mary," Bríghde told her, "this is no time for talking; it's time to do a good deed." "What's the news now, Bríghde?" Mary asked. "You surely must have heard the dreadful command that Herod has issued? I've come to see if I can think of any plan that will help you to save Little Jesus from the strait He's in." "God will help us, Bríghde," Mary answered. "Get ready so," said Bríghde, "and make no delay. Before daylight in the morning I will dress myself

17

in an *óinseach*'s rags and head for such and such a street. Maybe those on guard will follow me; if they do, face southward for the road that leads from the city and perhaps you'll succeed in crossing the bridge of the Great River before anyone challenges you. Goodbye now; I'll be off about my business."

'When Joseph came in Mary told him the whole story from start to finish. The following morning, as it was brightening for day, a terrible uproar could be heard outside. A foolish woman was decked out in straw and around her waist was a belt studded with lights and on her head was a ring with twelve candles lighting upon it. She made her way to the point most convenient for Mary to escape. She had a kind of a flute that made an odd sound: as she played the flute the guards were startled and when they raised their heads they saw the witless woman all lighted up. They went towards her, but she kept moving away before them like a gust of wind.

'As soon as Mary got the guards out of the way she set about making her way out of the city. Things went well for her until she came to the bridge across the Great River and there were two soldiers of the guard: they stood right before her on the crown of the road.

'"Where are you off to so early, decent woman?" one of them asked.

'"I've been a week in the city," Mary answered, "and my home is a good distance away. That's why I'm on the road so early."

'"What's that load you have on your back?' a soldier asked again.

'"A little lamb I got to rear as a pet."

'"Maybe this is an excuse," said the other soldier, seizing her and dragging her mantle off her. All he saw was a lamb, its four legs tied with a light cord.

'"See now; she's right," said the other soldier. "It's a great shame for us to delay her."

'Mary was walking on and on until she was free from danger; she sat down in a little corner under a green clump of bushes and lifted Jesus off her back. When she was rested she replaced Him on her back and some time later reached her destination. She now had the Infant safe; a few days afterwards there was appalling desolation and terror because of the slaughter of the little children of the city. The only sound to be heard was the sorrowful crying of the mothers whose children were being put to death by Herod the destroyer. When the dreadful scourge was over Bríghde went out to where Mary was and the pair of women were overjoyed at meeting each other again. They went on their knees and earnestly thanked God for having saved them. Mary could bestow no greater honour on Bríghde than to present her with a feast day. She did so in these words:

'"Your day will come before my day, Bríghde, until the end of the world."

'It has been thus ever since and Brighde's Day comes before Mary's Day and, since there were candles in the plan that Brighde thought of, candles are blessed in every church throughout the world; "Candlemas Day" it's called.'

Peig: the Autobiography of Peig Sayers of the Great Blasket Islands, 1974

THE CHRISTMAS PRESENTS

Maeve Binchy

Christmas Day, for Elizabeth, had always been an anti-climax; so much looked forward to, so much talked about, but when it came it always seemed to bring some disapproval, or some other cause for complaint which she would pretend not to notice. Last year it had been one long discussion about rationing and arguments about how they could possibly manage. Elizabeth thought that the Day with the O'Connors would be utterly perfect. She expected a story-book Christmas for the first time in her life.

For weeks they had all been making each other presents, and the cry of 'Don't come in!' arose whenever you went into a room unexpectedly. To Elizabeth's great surprise, Aisling talked enthusiastically about Santa Claus. Once or twice, Elizabeth had ventured a small doubt about him.

'Do you think that there actually might not be a Santa Claus, you know, the gifts might come from. . . somewhere else?'

'Don't be daft,' Aisling said. 'Sure, where else would they come from?' She had lit several candles asking God to remind Santa Claus of her requests.

Elizabeth had changed a great deal in her four months with the O'Connors. Once upon a time, she would have said nothing and just hoped that things would turn out for the best. Now, however, she felt able to intervene.

'Auntie Eileen?'

'Yes, darling?' Eileen was writing in the big household book she filled in every Saturday.

'I don't want to interfere but. . . you see, Aisling is praying to the Holy Family people in the church and asking them to tell Santa Claus that she wants a bicycle. . . and, you know. . . just. . . I thought you should know as well, if you see what I mean, just in case she doesn't tell you.'

Eileen pulled the child towards her affectionately. 'Now, that's very kind of you to tell me that,' she said.

'It's not that I'm asking you to buy expensive things like that, it's just that Aisling believes very strongly that what you tell Santa Claus should be a secret, and she mightn't tell you.'

'Well, I'll keep that information very carefully in my mind,' said Eileen solemnly. 'Run off with you, now.'

Christmas Eve was like a combination of Saturday nights with all the shoe polishing and neck washing, and the day of the Christmas play at school, all feverish excitement. Even grown-up people like Maureen and her friend Berna were giggling, and Young Sean was happy and wrapping up parcels.

During the night Elizabeth heard the door open. She glanced worriedly over at Aisling's bed but the red hair out on the pillow never stirred. Through half-closed eyes Elizabeth saw Sean place the bicycle, wrapped in brown paper and holly sprigs, at the end of Aisling's bed. And to her amazement she saw a similar shape coming to the end of her own bed. Two sharp trickles of tears began in her eyes. They were such a kind family, she would never be able to thank them. She must really try to explain to Mother in her next letter how kind they were. Please could she find words that wouldn't irritate Mother and make Mother feel that she was being criticised.

Then it was morning and there were screams of excitement as Aisling in pyjamas tore off the wrapping paper. As Elizabeth swung her legs out of bed, Aisling, her face flushed with happiness, came over and gave her a great hug. She forced herself to put her arms around Aisling too. Though this was a new experience and she was always nervous of something new. Up to now they had only linked arms when coming home from school. That had been the closest contact. But now it was a sea of affection and excitement and it almost drowned Elizabeth with its unfamiliarity.

But in no time there were shouts and calls, and squeaks and hoots on a trumpet, and more shouts. . .

'Down here in two minutes or Christmas or no Christmas you'll feel the palm of my hand!'

It was still dark as they went up the hill to the church calling and wishing people Happy Christmas. Several people asked Elizabeth what she got in her stocking. . . and Doctor Lynch, Berna's father, pinched her cheek and asked her was an Irish Christmas better than an English one. His wife pulled him away crossly.

There were sausages and eggs for breakfast, paper table napkins on the table. Niamh sat up in her high chair and gurgled at them. There was more suppressed excitement since presents were going to be given afterwards beside the fire. The big things had come in the night but the individual ones would come now, and then the girls could go out in the square with their bicycles, Maureen could parade with her new jacket and matching beret, Eamonn with his football and boots, Donal with his scooter. Then it would be in again for the huge goose that was already cooking in the range.

There were oohs and aahs over the presents, the pincushions, the bookmarks, the dish painted as an ashtray for Da, the necklace made of carefully threaded beads. But there was the greatest applause for the presents that Maureen gave. For Mam there was beautiful soap, and for Da there was a proper man's scarf. For Aisling and Elizabeth big bangles with coloured glass in them; for Eamonn a big light for his bicycle; for Donal a funny furry hat, and even for the baby a rattle. She had given her elder brother two matching hair brushes like gentlemen used in picture books, and for Peggy she had a sparkling brooch.

Maureen had been the last to do the distributing. She had asked if she could be and it seemed a glorious end to the present-giving. The air was so full of gratitude and re-examination of gifts that none of them except Elizabeth noted the anxious glances exchanged between Auntie Eileen and Uncle Sean. She couldn't interpret them – it was as if they alone had seen some hidden disaster. Uncle Sean evidently had decided to let Auntie Eileen deal with it, whatever it was. Elizabeth's face was reddening with anxiety, she knew it was.

'Right everyone, clear up all the mess, paper into this box, string into that, and *don't lose anything!*' Eileen supervised a huge sweep on the room. 'Now all of you out in the square, yes, you too, Sean, get a bit of exercise. . . and Donal, of course you can child. . . wrap up well. No, leave your furry hat here, that's the boy.'

In minutes she had the room cleared of people and presents. Elizabeth's heart pounded because she knew something was very wrong. She went into the kitchen with Peggy and helped to fold the paper up into squares. Peggy kept up a monologue about how much there was to be done for the meal and how little help anyone gave. . . but she was only muttering, and didn't expect any answer.

The voices came clearly from the next room.

'No, Maureen, sit down. Come on sit down. . .'

'I don't know what you mean Ma, what is it?'

'Maureen, where did you get the money to pay for these things. . . where?'

'Ma, I don't know what you mean. I saved up my pocket money like everyone else. . . of course I did Ma.'

'We're not fools Maureen. . . look at these things. They cost a fortune. That soap you bought your mother. . . it's fifteen shillings. I saw it myself in the chemist.'

'But Da, I didn't. . .'

'Just tell us where you got the money child, that's all your father and I want to know. Tell us quickly and don't ruin the day for all the rest of them.'

'I never took any of your money Mam, you can look in your desk, I didn't take a penny. . .'

'I didn't miss anything Sean.'

'And I didn't touch anything in your pocket, Da. . .'

'Come on, Maureen, you get a shilling a week, you have pounds worth of stuff here. Pounds and pounds. Can't you see your mother and I are heart-scalded over it. . .'

'Is this the thanks I get for giving you nice Christmas presents. . .'
Maureen had begun to cry. 'Is this. . . all. . . you. . . say accuse me of
stealing from you.'

'Well, the only other alternative. . . is that you stole from the shops.'
Eileen's voice was shaking as she voiced the suspicion.

'I *bought* them,' persisted Maureen.

'God almighty, those hair brushes you gave Sean, they're over two
pounds!' roared Sean. 'You're not leaving this room till we know.
Christmas dinner or no Christmas dinner. . . if I have to shake every
bone out of your body, I'll find out. Don't treat us like fools. *Bought* them
indeed. . .'

'You'll have to tell us sooner or later, your father is right. Tell us now.'

'I bought you Christmas presents to please you and this is all you
say. . .'

'I'm going to go up to Doctor Lynch's house and see whether their
family got fine presents from that Berna of theirs. Maybe the two of you
were in this together. Maybe Berna will tell us if you won't. . .'

'No!' it was a scream. 'No Da, don't go. Please don't go.'

There were sobs from Eileen, and shocked noises and wailings from
Maureen as well as her mother. There was the sound of great slappings
and a chair turning over. Elizabeth heard Aunt Eileen pleading with
Uncle Sean not to be so hard.

'Leave her, Sean, leave her till you calm down.'

'Calm down. Stealing from every other trader in the town. Into their
shops with that brat of a Lynch girl. Five shops, five families who've
done business with us for years and this brat goes in and steals from
them. Jesus Christ, what's there to be calm about. . . you're going in to
every one of them when the shops open. Every single one of them do
you hear, every item will be returned. And the Lynches will be told too,
mind that. They're not going to live in innocence over the pair of thieves
we have stalking the town. . .'

Elizabeth exchanged a fearful glance with Peggy as they heard another blow and another scream.

'Don't you be minding all that now,' said Peggy. 'Better not to poke
your nose into others' affairs. Better to hear nothing and say nothing.'

'I know,' said Elizabeth. 'But it's going to spoil Christmas.'

'Not at all,' said Peggy. 'We'll have a grand Christmas.'

'Ah, Da you can't hit a girl like that, stop it, Da, stop it!'

'Go away, Sean, I don't want you here, get out, it's my business.'

'Da, you can't hit Maureen like that, Ma stop him, he's hit her on the
head. Stop it, Da, stop it, you're too big, you'll kill her.'

Elizabeth fled from the kitchen and got her new bicycle. Round and
round the square she cycled, trying to brush the tears out of her eyes.
She didn't want the others to ask her what was wrong. She had no hope

that they would even get together for the goose now. Aunt Eileen had probably gone to the bedroom, Sean gone off out after the row with his father. Uncle Sean might have taken the keys and gone back into the store, and Maureen – heaven knew what would happen to Maureen. It was all turning out badly like everything always did. It was so unfair.

Light a Penny Candle, 1982

Christmas Hymn

GLORY to God in the highest,
  "Peace unto man, and good will;"
It broke when the dawning was nighest
  On the silence of pasture and hill.

When darkness was deepest in shadow,
  There burst forth a beautiful light
On sheep lying down in the meadow,
  And shepherds that watched them by night.

On heights by the Roman enslaved,
  On David's own Bethlehem town;
Yet here was a "greater than David,"
  But no man awoke, or looked down.

Great ones had thronged to the city,
  Had entered and fastened the door;
No room for the Virgin, no pity,
  For her, or the Child that she bore.

Their children lay shielded from danger,
  Close curtained, and cradled with care;
"This Babe ye shall find in a manger,"
  And none but the oxen were there.

Yet this was the promise of ages,
  The Wonderful, Counsellor, Son,
Whose name was on prophecy's pages,
  By whom our salvation is won.

Then hail we the Child in the manger,
  Creator, and Saviour, and King;
To Him shall the song of the stranger
  Their rarest and costliest bring.

And never, while Christians are living,
  The song of our Christmas shall cease;
To God shall be praise and thanksgiving,
  To man shall be pardon and peace.

                    MRS. ALEXANDER.

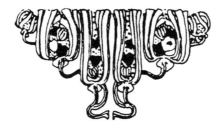

POTEEN FOR SALE

Tim Daly

It was the last market day before Christmas in the little town of Ballower and there was great confusion. The town was thronged with mountain men and women. They had donkeys and carts, turkeys and geese, ducks and chickens. The men were clad in snow-white *báiníns*, black soft hats or grey caps. The women wore grey shawls and scarlet petticoats, the length of the petticoat roughly indicating the age of the wearer. The range being from the knee to the ankle. Orange coloured carts, and bright blue creels, all added to a magnificent splash of colour at its best in the morning sun that was quickly thawing out the night's frost. Everybody was busy buying or selling.

It was the one day in the year there was traffic congestion in the town and Sergeant Logan was a bit flustered trying to keep the road clear of donkey-carts. On market days throughout the year he allowed one of the three Guards under him to deal with the traffic. But this was an abnormal situation which called for the attention of the officer in charge of the area.

I had been up early that morning and walked three miles from home in the hope of meeting a buyer for the poteen I had distilled. I arrived in the town without a clue as to where I might find somebody who would buy. For some reason I find it hard to understand my late father never told me how to go about selling poteen. He gave me lots of instruction in distilling, but never a word about the sale.

In previous years he went to the market, returned home, and told us that he had met a man who bought the poteen; but he never told me that for months he had been making discreet inquiries. Often I had heard him ask neighbours how their sons and daughters were doing in England. Were they coming home for Christmas? Then the conversation would take a more general turn, and other people's names would be mentioned. 'Be gob, he's getting a little bit long in the tooth. Any notion of getting married?' Gossipy kind of talk. Later I discovered that this is the way to find your customers. When people are coming home for

Christmas there are hooleys. Even some of the more sophisticated townspeople, who offer their guests nothing less expensive than whiskey, might like to stretch it a bit by mixing it with a little poteen. A couple of weddings in a parish is a godsend to a distiller.

I wandered aimlessly down the street. Rows of donkeys and carts on either side of me. Inside the high creels I could see turkeys, geese, and ducks. Some of them had their long necks stuck out between the rails struggling desperately for freedom. Others were lying quietly and making the best of their misfortune.

Sergeant Logan was outside the barracks and when he saw me coming he put his thumbs inside the belt of his tunic, and began tapping the ends of his enormous fingers against his shining chrome-plated buckle. As he might say himself, he was observing me. I hated the sight of the bastard. Only for him and his three Guards life would be comparatively easy.

'Come here, you,' he said.

I walked over to him.

'What's your name?'

'John McEnley.'

'There's a little matter I'd like to discuss with you. Would you mind coming inside?'

'Certainly,' I said, knowing I had no option but to agree.

A short, middle-aged man dressed in a grey cap, faded *báinín* and patched home-spun pants, came up the street leading a donkey-and-cart.

'Just a moment,' said the sergeant to this man.

He pulled up the donkey and an expression of either surprise or fear crept over his unshaven face.

I waited at the door of the barracks.

The sergeant pointed to a spot on the shaft of the cart about at the donkey's hind-quarters.

'Do you not know the law requires you to have your name and address on the shaft of your cart?'

The shabby little man took an old blackened pipe with an extremely short shank out of his mouth and spat on the road.

'But, Sergeant, my name and my address are on the shaft.'

The sergeant looked closer. 'It's not legible. It does not fulfil the requirements of the law. Get it done before you meet me again.'

'I will, I will, Sergeant. Hup, hup, Judy,' he said to the ass.

The sergeant motioned me to move into the barracks.

I obeyed.

'What have you in your pockets?'

'Nothing, Sergeant.'

'It couldn't be less. Are you sure you're not carrying poteen?'

'I'm certain.' I opened my frieze overcoat. He felt round my hips.

'Where are you from?'

'Rushvalley.'

'What are you doing in town today?'

'I came in to buy a few things for Christmas.'

'What kind of things?'

'Some groceries and things for the house.'

'Is there no one at home but yourself?'

'And my mother.'

'And why didn't your mother buy some groceries and things for the house?' he said, mimicking my mountain accent.

'She has the 'flu. She wasn't able to come to town.'

One thing I was always rather good at was telling lies.

'Show me the money you have for buying the groceries and the things for the house?'

Sixpence was all the money I had, but I never believed in admitting anything until I was proved guilty. I shoved my hand into my trouser pocket as if I expected to find pounds. Nothing there. I searched the other pocket. Took out the sixpence and left it on the table. Then I searched my waistcoat pockets. I returned to the trouser pockets, searching furiously.

'Great God, I've lost it!' I said. 'What on earth are we going to do? We won't have a penny to buy anything for Christmas.'

I searched the pockets of my overcoat. Took if off and threw it on the floor. Turned my trouser pockets inside out. I was really agitated. Almost weeping.

'How much had you?' the sergeant asked.

'Two pounds, Sergeant. Holy Lord, my mother'll starve. I can't get a day's work. I can't even get home assistance before Christmas.'

Guard Meehan came in and looked at me. 'What's wrong with this fellow, Sergeant?' he said.

The sergeant told him.

'Do you think he ever had the money, Sergeant?'

'I don't know. That act could be mountain honesty or animal cunning. It's not easy to know one from the other. You may go, McEnley,' he said.

I put on my overcoat and took the sixpence off the table. I was still searching my pockets and moaning and muttering to myself as I went out the door. . .

Women with grey shawls and red petticoats lugged heavy baskets. *Báinín*ed men carried sacks of flour and meal.

Members of the wandering tribe known as The Tinkers made a general nuisance of themselves either begging or pestering people to buy little odds-and-ends such as religous goods, hairpins, collar-studs and boot-thongs. Sometimes women bought articles they didn't want because they were afraid a refusal might provoke the wrath of these foul-mouthed primitives who got their name from their chief occupation – making and mending tin vessels.

A cheap-jack selling women's clothing was amusing his audience with double-meaning obscenity. Mountain women, draped from head to heel in grey shawls and red petticoats – the type you'd associate with rosary beads and a string of religous objects – were gathered round him, breaking their sides laughing at the smut that was rolling gracefully off his tongue.

A trick-o'-the loop had a lucky loop and an unlucky loop. A fortune-teller was ready to get cracking on anyone who'd cross her palm with silver, and a three-card-trickster offered a quid to whoever could find the lady.

A band struck up beside a quack dentist's tent. It only played when he got a patient, and the louder the patient roared the more the band played.

The chances of selling poteen were slim. I finished eating my loaf, and wondered what on earth I was going to do.

The Mountain Man, 1960

HOME FOR CHRISTMAS

Norman Dugdale

The people I encounter in the street
Have hardly changed. Pinched by cold, eyes dulled
By small defeats, mouths thin drawn
Less in bitterness than resignation,
They are cumbersome and patient as slow cattle.
Yes, I have seen them all before. But then
They belonged to my parents' generation,
Now to mine – done for, like this raw
And windy town among the Pennines, stone-faced
Still, although its looms stopped long ago.

Running Repairs, 1983

AN IRISH CHRISTMAS

Maud E. Sargent

By the time December, or 'the Month of the New-Born', as its Irish name means, begins, much excitement may be noticed through the length and breadth of Green Erin, even in remote hamlets along the coast, and in scattered farms and cabins dotted over the wide turf-bogs, the heathery hills, and the romantic glens of 'the distressful country'.

'The vanithee' is busy fattening turkeys and geese, fowls and ducks for the markets which take place shortly before Christmas – perhaps a fortnight earlier, for many of the birds are destined to cross the Channel and furnish a Christmas dinner for 'the Sassenach'.

Ere dawn on the market day long strings of 'butts', as the springless wooden carts of Munster are called, wind along the roads, accompanied by a chorus of gobbling, hissing, and cackling. The birds are squeezed into huge baskets, or tied in couples by the legs, and laid beside the women, who, enveloped in black or blue hood-cloaks, with gay shawls and handkerchiefs tied over their heads outside the snowy-frilled caps, are seated on 'a wisp o' stray' in the bottom of the cart, which does not boast of a seat. The good man sits in front to drive, his legs dangling beside the shafts, as he jerks the reins, and strikes the horse, jennet, or donkey with a whip or ashplant, bidding him 'Go on out o' that', or exchanges cheery greetings with anybody he meets – often giving a lift to people walking to the market town.

A calf or pig often sits 'like a Christian' in the straw beside his mistress, adding his share of noise to the poultry-yard chorus. Nowadays the younger women are beginning to discard the picturesque cloaks, caps, and short full skirts of serge or homespun for would-be fashionable costumes and hats of every colour in the rainbow. In spite of their fine array, however, the pig and fowls usually continue to share their equipage, and the dresses are tucked up carefully, displaying the ample petticoats of red or white flannel dear to the hearts of country-women.

Reaching their destination, they climb out of the butts, lift down the great baskets as though they were a feather-weight, or carry a pair of birds in each hand – the wretched creatures hanging head downwards.

People slightly higher in the social scale drive to market on 'the side-car' – the possession of one is a strong proof of gentility – and send the pigs to market in a creel, driven by a servant, or by 'one o' the boys', as the unmarried men of the family are called without the least regard to age. The fowls, however, are sure to have a place on the car, with the fresh eggs and the rolls of creamy butter for which Cork and Limerick are so famous.

While most of these things are for sale, some are meant for Christmas boxes to customers or friends, for while the peasants have a keen eye to a bargain, and will haggle over every halfpenny in such transactions, they are very generous in other respects, and never forget 'a complimint' at the festive season for 'the quality' or the shopkeepers with whom they deal, and do not forget their kinsfolk to the most remote degree, for they are as clannish as the Scotch.

Beggars, too, may be sure of 'an alms' just now. Accordingly at Christmas they appear in crowds in the towns and villages, and along the roads, entering farm-house and cabin with the pious greeting, 'God save all here', to which the inmates reply, 'God save ye kindly!'

These wanderers are of all sorts and kinds, in every stage of rags and tatters, though some of them are really comfortably off – mendicancy is rather a lucrative profession in Ireland, especially for 'afflicted crathurs', who are supposed to be under the special protection of heaven, so the blind, the dumb, the cripple, and the idiot are rarely refused something – perhaps a handful of potatoes or turnips, 'a dust o' tay', a head of cabbage, a chunk of griddle-cake, or some feathers to stuff a pillow or mattress – 'a handsome feather-bed' is the great ambition of poor people, who carefully collect down for the purpose, and the recent order against bringing these articles to America caused great dissatisfaction to emigrants.

The beggars carry bags, or wallets, and formidable sticks, the latter used principally to keep off the dogs, who do not regard ragged folks with favour in any country. As it is thought unlucky to refuse charity to cripples or half-witted persons at any time, and particularly so at Christmas, 'Judy-the-Rags', 'Paddy-on-the-Sticks', and 'Mike-the-Fool' are likely to get a good supply of food and money on their rounds, and the police leave them alone, unless they happen to be overcome by a few more 'drops o' the crathur' than even their well-seasoned heads can stand. Some of the wanderers are peddlars, ballad-singers, or music-ians, as well as the news-carriers and messengers of remote districts – to say nothing of their acting as match-makers when Shrovetide, the season for peasant marriages, is at hand! They are welcome in the scattered dwellings on mountain side or wild seashore, far from town or railway, and a bed is often kept ready for such chance visitors. Only a corner in the barn, perhaps, or the wide settle in the chimney-corner, but either will prove acceptable on a winter night, and wretched as some of these wanderers are, it is almost unheard of for one of them to abuse the kindness of his host by stealing or doing any mischief. Farmers often say it is wiser to give such people shelter than to run the risk of their setting the ricks on fire, or helping themselves to poultry etc., if left to prowl about out of doors, but the true explanation of the custom is the belief which lingers even yet that the saints often come back to earth – especially at Christmas – in the form of beggars, and that those who refuse alms and shelter to a poor wanderer run the risk of missing the blessings which attend those who thus 'entertain angels unawares!'

They frequent fairs and markets, and get many a copper after the produce is sold, and the farmers and their rosy, cheery wives prepare to 'bring home the Christmas' in the shape of such unwonted luxuries as a piece of fresh meat – pig's head and bacon are the only meat eaten by the average country-folks on ordinary occasions, for the standard of comfort is low, especially with regard to food, and butcher's meat is a rarity. If they are well-to-do, there may be the materials for a pudding in the basket, and a bottle of 'sherry wine', in case any 'ginteel' visitors should look in during the holidays. The good woman will have a parcel of groceries of better quality than those sold at 'the shop', which is to be found in every village, or at the nearest cross-roads, and a 'barmbrack' (spotted loaf), the orothodox Christmas cake, full of currants, candied-peel, and spice, and sometimes containing a ring, and a few loaves of white bread, still regarded as holiday fare in the country, where soda-bread, baked in a 'bastable-oven' on the open hearth, is the everyday food. A bottle of whiskey will not be forgotten, nor a few 'sweeties' for the children, while the grocer, or chandler, will have presented a Christmas candle, burned at this season in Munster and Connaught, as well as in many parts of Eastern Europe, as it formerly was in England. It is lighted on Christmas Eve, when it is set in a scooped-out turnip – few people have a candlestick large enough to hold it, as it weighs at least a pound, and is very thick. The turnip is artfully hidden by frills of cut paper and sprigs of evergreens, and is set on the kitchen table. The great taper is generally lit by the master of the house, though in Kerry the rule is that a man named 'John', or a woman called 'Mary', must light it, after blessing it in the Name of the Holy Trinity. It is allowed to burn all night on Christmas Eve, sometimes on Christmas Day, and invariably on New Year's Eve, and the Eve of the Epiphany, known in Ireland as 'The Women's Christmas' and 'Little Christmas'. Woe is said to befall the house where the candle has gone out before the winter dawn creeps up over the dark hills and lonely bogs.

It is usual to sit up all night on Christmas Eve. Pious folk go to the Midnight Mass, and come home to eat the Christmas Eve supper of salt fish and potatoes. Then they gather round the fire, drinking punch, and talking of 'the good ould ancient times', before the Famine, when the fairies were common in the land – the bright days before America had drawn the flower of Ireland's youth across 'the salt say!' Perhaps those old days were not so much better than our modern ones, for an Irish proverb reminds us that 'Cows far off have long horns', but certainly harmless mirth and ready wit seem dying out of the country with the

ancient customs, so many of which are fading into oblivion.

Songs are sung and games played by the fire-light, and boys and girls dance on the earthen floor, or slip out of doors to try some of the odd spells associated with Christmas Eve, for just before midnight on that date is said to be the best time in the year for searching into futurity.

Bold spirits will even venture to visit cowhouse and stable. For the cow, the sheep, the horse, and the ass are holy and blessed beasts, because they were in the stable at Bethlehem on the first Christmas Eve; and the donkey is twice blessed because Our Lord rode on him as He entered Jerusalem, and ever since the animal's back is marked with the Cross, and at twelve o'clock the beast kneels to worship the new-born Babe, and those who see the wonderful sight and touch the Cross at that moment will gain their heart's desires!. . . Domestic animals and poultry are usually given extra food on Christmas Day – a custom which prevails in many countries, and is supposed to bring good luck to the farm during the coming year.

Vigorous house-cleaning takes place for the Christmas; walls are white-washed, boards scrubbed, hollows in the earthen floor filled up, windows cleaned, and the tins, candlesticks, and gay plates, dishes, cups, and jugs on the big dresser are polished till they shine. The wide chimney is swept – no easy job where professional sweeps and long brushes are unknown, but 'Necessity is the Mother of Invention!' Sometimes a goose is sent flying down the chimney to dislodge the soot; sometimes a brush is made of a furze or holly bush, tied in the middle of a rope long enough to reach from the hearth to the top of the chimney. One end is held by a person who stands on the roof, the other is grasped by someone standing on the hearth, and the 'fuzz-bush' is hauled up and down till every atom of soot is rubbed off, and if a good portion of it has descended on the open hearth and the person standing beneath, well, 'Clane dirt is no poison!'

There are few waits and carol-singers in Ireland, but the 'Wren-Boys' still go about on St Stephen's Day, and in some parts of the country the Mummers linger even now. In Meath they go about in bands of about fourteen on St Stephen's Day fantastically dressed, and led by 'Rune Rhyme', who knocks at every door, and asks permission for his followers to enter:

> Here come I, 'Rune Rhyme' – give me room to rhyme,
> Till I show my activity at Christmastime!
> To the sound of the horn, the beat of the drum!
> We are the jolly Mummers who at Christmas come;
> We are the jolly Mummers who walk the street,
> We are the jolly Mummers who please all we meet!
> If you don't believe what I say,
> Enter 'The Wren', and clear the way!

The Wren comes in, followed in turn by 'The Queen', 'Tom Fool', 'Beelzebub', an inferior demon 'Little Devil', or 'Devil D'Out', 'Oliver Cromwell', whose reputation in Ireland rivals that of Beelzebub; 'St Patrick', 'St George', borrowed from the English Mummers; 'The Doctor', 'Slack', 'Terry Thatcher', and other curious personages. The bad characters in the time-honoured drama are conquered by the saints. St George, however, is killed, and restored to life by a salve and potion applied by the Doctor, and after a number of combats, interspersed with songs and dances, which have been practised assiduously for weeks, the Mummers all take hands, and execute a sort of reel, during which Tom Fool strikes his staff and bladder on the heads and backs of all who come in his way, as he has done during the performance of the play, just as his namesake did in the Miracle Plays of mediaeval times, from which our Mummers are derived.

After this the Mummers receive money or eatables, and sometimes go on at once to another house, but if there is a party assembled in the first dwelling they visit, they join in the dances and games with the other young folks, 'taking the floor' with the prettiest 'colleens', each couple trying to dance the others down.

New Ireland Review, 1910

THE RUSHING OF BELFAST BARRACKS, 1770

Francis Joseph Bigger

Matters came to a head with a farmer named David Douglas, who was the reputed leader of the resistance in Templepatrick. On Friday, 21 December, 1770, Douglas was arrested in Belfast by Waddell Cunningham, and lodged in the military barracks. The charge against him was houghing cattle belonging to Thomas Greg, of Belfast, who, with Waddell Cunningham, was a particular object of dislike on account of the lands they had taken over the tenants' heads. The Steelboys determined to rescue Douglas. On Sunday, the 23, a band of them marched to Templepatrick meeting-house while service was being held, and summoned their comrades to join them. It is said they rapped the butts of their rifles against the door, calling the men to come out, as that was no place for men at such a time, but might do for the women. They then marched to Belfast, gathering reinforcements as they went.

They met at a house on the shore road, called the Stag's Head, at Skegoneill, where their number amounted to about 1,200 men, chiefly from Templepatrick, Doagh, Ballyclare, and Carnmoney. Here they were formed into regular order by an old soldier called Nathaniel Matthews. They were led by Gordy Crawford on horseback who carried before him several iron crow-bars rolled in hay ropes for the purpose of breaking open doors and gates. On news of their advance, Stewart Banks, the sovereign, and many other men, fled to the military barracks for protection. The Hearts of Steel, armed with guns, pistols, swords, scythes, pitchforks, etc., at once surrounded the barracks, and demanded Douglas's release. This was refused. The Hearts of Steel then

36

proceeded to the house of Waddell Cunningham, which stood on the site of the present Provincial Bank, in Royal Avenue, Belfast, broke in the door, and began to wreck the furniture. Dr Haliday approached the raiders, and exhorted them to desist. They promised to do so if he would procure the release of Douglas. With this intention Dr Haliday set out for the military barracks, but when the soldiers saw the crowd again approaching, they fired, killing several and wounding more, amongst the killed being William Russell, Carnmoney; Andrew Cristy, Donegore; and J. Sloan, Falls.

The renewed violence of the raiders convinced Stewart Banks, the sovereign, that the most expedient course was to release the prisoner, for, during the long parley, the Hearts of Steel had become impatient. They set fire to Waddell Cunningham's house, and fired shots into Thomas Greg's. This destruction, and the fear lest the entire town should be burned as the whole place was in an uproar, had the desired effect. At one o'clock in the morning [24 December] the barrack gates were thrown open and Douglas was restored to his friends, who marched him back in triumph 'between Cave Hill and the sea,' to Templepatrick.

The Ulster Land War, 1910

TURKEYS OBSERVED

Seamus Heaney

One observes them, one expects them;
Blue-breasted in their indifferent mortuary,
Beached bare on the cold marble slabs
In immodest underwear frills of feather.

The red sides of beef retain
Some of the smelly majesty of living:
A half-cow slung from a hook maintains
That blood and flesh are not ignored.

But a turkey cowers in death.
Pull his neck, pluck him, and look –
He is just another poor forked thing,
A skin bag plumped with inky putty.

He once complained extravagantly
In an overture of gobbles;
He lorded it on the claw-flecked mud
With a grey flick of his Confucian eye.

Now, as I pass the bleak Christmas dazzle,
I find him ranged with his cold squadrons:
The fuselage is bare, the proud wings snapped,
The tail-fan stripped down to a shameful rudder.

Death of a Naturalist, 1966

REALITY BREAKING IN

Frank O'Connor

Father had a half-day on Christmas Eve, and came home at noon with his week's pay in his pocket – that is, when he got home at all. Mother and I knew well how easily he was led astray by out-of-works who waited at the street corners for men in regular jobs, knowing that on Christmas Eve no one could refuse them a pint. But I never gave that aspect of it much thought. It wasn't for anything so commonplace as Father's weekly pay that I was waiting. I even ignored the fact that when he did come in, there was usually an argument and sometimes a quarrel. At ordinary times when he did not give Mother enough to pay the bills, she took it with resignation, and if there was a row it was he who provoked it by asking: 'Well, isn't that enough for you?' But at Christmas she would fight and fight desperately.

One Christmas Eve he came home and handed her the housekeeping money with a complacent air, and she looked at the coins in her hand and went white. 'Lord God, what am I to do with that?' I heard her whisper despairingly, and I listened in terror because she never invoked the name of God. Father suddenly blew up into the fury he had been cooking up all the way home – a poor, hard-working man deprived of his little bit of pleasure at Christmas time because of an extravagant wife and child. 'Well, what do you want it for?' he snarled. 'What do I want it for?' she asked distractedly, and went through her shopping list, which, God knows, must have been modest enough. And then he said something that I did not understand, and I heard her whispering in reply, and there was a frenzy in her voice that I would not have believed possible; 'Do you think I'll leave him without it on the one day of the year?'

Years later I suddenly remembered the phrase because of its beauty, and realized that it was I who was to be left without a toy, and on this one day of the year that seemed to her intolerable. And yet I did not allow it to disturb me; I had other expectations, and I was very happy when the pair of us went shopping together, down Blarney Lane, past the shop in the big old house islanded in Goulnaspurra, where they sold the coloured cardboard cribs I coveted, with shepherds and snow, manger and star, and across the bridge to Myles's Toy Shop on the North Main Street. There in the rainy dusk, jostled by prams and drunken women in shawls, and thrust on one side by barefooted children from the lanes, I stood in wonder, thinking which treasure Santa Claus would bring me from the ends of the earth to show his appreciation of the way I had behaved in the past twelve months. As he was a most superior man, and I a most superior child, I saw no limit to the possibilities of the period, and no reason why Mother should not join in my speculations.

It was usually dark when we tramped home together, up Wyse's Hill, from which we saw the whole city lit up beneath us and the trams reflected in the water under Patrick's Bridge; or later – when we lived in Barrackton, up Summerhill, Mother carrying the few scraps of meat and the plum pudding from Thompson's and me something from the Penny Bazaar. We had been out a long time, and I was full of expectations of what the postman might have brought in the meantime. Even when he hadn't brought anything, I didn't allow myself to be upset, for I knew that the poor postmen were dreadfully overworked at this time of year. And even if he didn't come later, there was always the final Christmas morning delivery. I was an optimistic child, and the holly over the mirror in the kitchen and the red paper in the lighted window of the huxter shop across the street assured me that the Christmas numbers were right and anything might happen.

There were lesser pleasures to look forward to, like the lighting of the Christmas candle and the cutting of the Christmas cake. As the youngest of the household I had the job of lighting the candle and saying solemnly: 'The light of heaven to our souls on the last day,' and Mother's principal worry was that before the time came Father might slip out to the pub and spoil the ritual, for it was supposed to be carried out by the oldest and the youngest, and Father, by convention, was the oldest, though, in fact, as I later discovered, he was younger than Mother.

In those days the cake and candle were supposed to be presented by the small shopkeeper from whom we bought the tea, sugar, paraffin oil, and so on. We could not afford to shop in the big stores where everything was cheaper, because they did not give credit to poor people, and most of the time we lived on credit. But each year our 'presents' seemed to grow smaller and Mother would comment impatiently on the meanness of Miss O' or Miss Mac in giving us a tiny candle or a stale cake. (When the 1914 War began they stopped giving us the cake.) Mother could never believe that people could be so mean, but where we were concerned, they seemed to be capable of anything. The lighted candle still left me with two expectations. However late it grew I never ceased to expect the postman's knock, and even when that failed, there was the certainty that Christmas morning would set everything right.

But when I woke on Christmas morning, I felt the season of imagination slipping away from me and the world of reality breaking in. If all Santa Claus could bring me from the North Pole was something I could have bought in Myles's Toy Shop for a couple of pence, he seemed to me to be wasting his time. Then the postman came, on his final round before a holiday that already had begun to seem eternal, and either he brought nothing for us, or else he brought the dregs of the Christmas mail, like a Christmas card from somebody who had just got Mother's card and remembered her existence at the last moment. Often, even this would be in an unsealed envelope and it would upset her for hours. It was strange in a woman to whom a penny was money that an unsealed envelope seemed to her the worst of ill-breeding, equivalent to the small candle or the stale cake – not a simple measure of economy, but plain, unadulterated bad taste.

An Only Child, 1961

THE STAR

Joseph Campbell

Thro' the roaring boughs of sin
Burns a solitary star.
It is of the cherubin,
It has all the joys that are;
Burning thro' the roaring boughs,
On the horn of heaven's house.

Black the boughs against the air;
White the star, and cherub-fair.

Hooded owls make ceaseless moan
Thro' the sin-excited boughs.
On the golden finial-stone
Crowning heaven's purple house
Burns the star – remote, unstirred,
Steadfast. . . beacon of the Word.

Pedlar's Pack

A DUBLIN CHRISTMAS, 1949

Micheál Mac Liammóir

December 24   Almost unbroken succession of friends and parties. Had lunch with Kate O'Brien back from New York, where her new play, *That Lady* with Cornell, had filthy press and is doing good business. Kate handsomer and grander than ever.

We have acquired new car called Humber Hawk (pale green) and in it went to visit my aunt Craven, also Shelah Richards, Jack Dunne, and others, and tonight shopped. Sacred annual mission to Moore Street accomplished, leaving car in large patch of trampled cabbage leaves while we bought holly, Christmas candle, and some ferocious ornaments for the Tree, also large bottle of Rum, as this year intended, as usual, to be what Tallulah Bankhead described in brief chat on the subject to Orson as A Real Old Fashioned Christmas.

Went home to our Christmas Eve party, into and out of which everyone in Dublin seemed to drop; very successful. Also joined by nieces Sally and Mary Rose; the latter slipped out to Midnight Mass and returned, looking elevated, to sleep on sofa by drawing-room fire with reinstated Siamese cat Rachel. Denis Johnston and Betty most expert and severely surrealist at new game taught us by Orson in St Paul and now spreading wildely through Dublin. Erskine Childers a trifle Pragmatical in approach, but *sound*. (You know my methods, Watson.)

All the gin disappeared. Hope some Tavern or other will be open tomorrow.

December 25   All went well (though overwhelmingly oversized turkey also slightly overcooked round legs in excitement and rather heartlessly christened St Joan by Hilton). Everyone pleased with presents, also with lighted Tree (microscopic and wrong shape), which caught fire but caused no damage, and dear Barty gave us beautiful books of her own childhood in the '80's, illustrated by Walter Crane, Jacob Hood, and Kate Greenaway. Howth in the evening: McMaster cottage shut up owing to absence in Australia. Missed Mac and my sister Mana badly. Telephone talks with Marjory Hawtrey (London) and Orson (Paris). Marjory in almost Dickensian Christmas mood and thinks Life Worth While; O. in pain with his (Spanish Lady) hand, God help him.

Put Money in thy Purse, 1952

43

GETTIN' A GERRL UP THE BACK LANE

Brendan O'Byrne

The wren, the wren the king of all birds,
Saint Stephenses Day he was caught in the furze.

It was the morning after Christmas and the dirty-faced urchins, dressed in anything they could lay their hands on, stood in turn outside each door brandishing a holly branch and impudently pretending that a wren was hidden somewhere among the leaves. A country custom somehow preserved in the slums where no decent wren would ever be seen, it raised a few shillings and countless slices of cold plum pudding for the Wren Boys as they remorselessly flogged the last vestige of goodwill from the festivities.

'Are ya spin-spout or black-out, Larry?' asked Titia Paderewski as she stopped him outside her own house on the corner of Wilson Place.

'Spin-spout,' answered Larry. 'Why?'

She gave him a womanish look. 'I thought mebbe y' were black-out with me yesterdee,' she complained. 'Ya never kem next, nigh nor near me.'

'Aw, I wuz busy,' he answered with startling originality. 'Me scoother's broke,' he added, as if that explained everything. The scooter was already a thing of the past and now lay in the backyard of Number Four with one wheel buckled and the footboard hanging loose for want of a screw which no one in that house would ever fix.

'I've got somethin' for ya,' Titia continued, and she produced the tie-pin and carefully stuck it in the lapel of his jacket, standing back a pace to admire her work afterwards.

'Jaysus!' breathed Larry. 'That's a luvvely pin, Titia. Thanks very much.'

'I think it suits ya,' she said in a satisfied tone of voice as he gloried in the sweet stench of Kolene from his greased hair. 'I got that special for you, Larry. Did ya get anythin' for me?'

'A course I did!' he protested, although the thought had never even entered his head. 'I got ya somethin' special too.'

'What is it, Larry?' asked the half-pint Cleopatra. 'Somethin' nice!'

'Yes,' he blustered. 'It was a. . . a. . .' (his eye lighted on the slide confining the dark mass of her hair at the back of her head) 'it wuz a slide, like a buttherfly it wuz. But it got broke.'

'Sure that's no matter, Larry,' she said comfortably. 'Ya can easy get me another. There's a luvvely wan in Geoghan's for sixpence.'

'Aye,' he agreed, dejectedly, 'I'll get ya that wan so,' as he wondered where the sixpence was going to come from, for, although there had been a lot of money around during the past week, Larry was not of the saving kind and money usually only stayed in his pocket for as long as it took to get to the nearest sweetshop. But maybe Daddy would take him on the traditional St Stephen's Day visits to friends to take a slice of cold pudding and sip a little wine. Kids didn't get the wine, of course, but sometimes they got a wing or two instead. In no time at all he'd have the sixpence for her feckin' hair-slide, if it stopped at that – because he had a feeling that having a mott could turn out to be a very expensive business in the long run.

Titia's foreign eyes glistened like shiny pieces of coal. 'Are ya comin' up the back lane tonight?' she asked, and a sudden panic assailed Larry for events were moving much too fast for him.

'I can't,' he answered. 'We'll all be in the house.'

'So'll we,' she countered. 'But ya could slip out for a minnut at fivea clock. It'll be nice an' dark then.'

So at five of the clock that evening, and after much elaborate stretching and yawning, Larry told his parents that he felt like having a bit of a walk around the block and Daddy and Mammy shared a glance of secret understanding, for he was not usually a lad given to explaining his movements and especially not in advance. Two minutes later he uttered an expletive that a lad of his age should not have known as his foot slithered in someone's mess in the back lane. Beyond the detritus of Wilson and Wentworth Place, and at the dead end of the lane between two high walls, a faint glimmer of white showed where Titia was waiting for her lover.

Now at last they were together and alone in darkness and he was at a complete loss to know what to do next. 'Gettin' a gerrl up the back lane' was a phrase much used by his contemporaries as something promising unimaginable delights, but none of them had ever as much as hinted what you did with them when you got them there. Larry approached his love gingerly, lifting each foot in great deliberation for fear of getting more mess on his new boots and wishing to Jaysus he had had enough sense to tell her that he just did not want to go up the back lane with her (or with anyone else for that matter), and they'd both get the skelpin' of their lives if their parents ever found out, for the back lane after dark was what the priests would call 'an occasion of sin', and no decent girl was ever seen coming out of it however blameless she may have been when she went in. To the good people hereabouts the opportunity pre-supposed the deed. As he came near her Titia leaned her face towards him and he leaned his face towards her and planted a slobbery kiss on her left eyebrow. Then, with his duty done, he turned to go before any of the oul' wans caught them and beat the devil outa him. A snatch of song from the end of Grant's Row unnerved him completely and he briefly thought of scrambling over the wall and out through one of the houses in Wentworth Place and then as far away from this accursed spot as his legs would carry him. Later on he would think of some excuse for his parents. Always he seemed to be thinking of excuses for someone or other, and if it wasn't for his Daddy and Mammy or Brother Haggerty it was for bloody Titia or even Tommy Fitz. Inadequate as he felt, the panic came first and he crouched to make his first effort to scale the wall but Titia wasn't having that, not after all this time and all the trouble she had taken with her sister's Phul Nana and Tokalone an' gettin' here early an' everythin'. Her two small hands caught him firmly on either side of his face and her lips forced themselves against his and stayed there for a full second while a trembling warmth flooded through him to make his thighs tingle and his foot beat a manic tattoo beyond his controlling. Then a fear of the unknown overwhelmed him and he rushed out of the lane towards the familiar safety of his own home.

A little later Titia followed him: a smiling Titia thinking to herself that Larry was going to be all right. He was just a bit slow, that was all.

Wilson Place, 1984

A BITTER-SWEET CHRISTMAS

Michael O'Beirne

It was only a few days to Christmas and I had been shopping. Hurrying home I rushed upstairs with a square cardboard box, stole quietly into the bedroom to be alone, placed the box on a bed, I removed the lid and for the first time really saw my concertina. It was of reddish glossy wood, a compact octagonal shape with leather hand-supports. Carefully prised from its box the concertina relaxed on my knees, stretching itself with a happy little sigh.

Immediately I propped up the tutor and began to practise the first tune, 'Home Sweet Home'. You didn't have to understand a note of music, it showed which button to press: One *Two*, One Two *One*, One Two *One* One, Two, Three, Four. Each button played two different notes, depending on whether you made the concertina suck in air or blow it out. My tutor even gave the words:

Where e'er—you may—wan—der, there's no—o place—like home;
Be it—ev—er so hum—ble, there's—no place—like—home. . .

Like my mouth-organ before it, the concertina was not greatly appreciated. Even my mother, always especially gay at a time of full and plenty, lost patience and scolded: 'Oh, for God's sake shut up with that!'

I'd noticed how people at this time could change, and like in *A Christmas Carol*, become good and kind. Of course it was the birthday of the Baby Jesus. Maybe that was why nearly everybody seemed to feel a special glow that made the cold, dark days less dark and cold.

I remember this Christmas Eve well. Miss McCarthy's shop window had all coloured lights around it, and when I went in lots of people were there buying big boxes of chocs and everything. The lights in the shop glittered on a row of frosty Father Christmases. I'd been sent down for a bar of chocolate but Miss McCarthy said to wait. When the people had gone she stooped under the counter and handed me an oblong box. I knew by its picture that it was a train. She held it towards me.

'For Christmas,' she said, very pleased. Then her face changed. She must have seen that I looked disappointed.

'Oh dear. I'm wrong,' she said. 'That's not for you at all.' She stooped out of sight again and reappeared beaming. '*There's* your present!' It was a book called *Prester John*, by John Buchan.

Never before had I been given such a thrilling gift. The title of one chapter was the name of a place in South Africa that was the longest name ever, it went across the page: Blaauwildebeesteafontain. I had read books before, and had listened to books being read out, but never had I known a story quite like this. It seemed too real to be a story. But how could I know whether it was real or not? It must be because I was stupid that I felt so puzzled and frustrated.

'Was Prester John a real man, Maggie?' I asked anxiously, coming into the little room on Christmas morning.

'Prester John? Is that the book you got from Miss McCarthy? Look, Mazie.' Maggie held the book up to show the cover – a tall black man in a white robe. 'Wasn't that a nice present she gave him?'

'But was he real, Maggie? A real man?'

She was looking at the cover with her glasses on, reading what it said there in a kind of mutter: 'Prester, another word for priest. He was a legendary figure, king and high-priest in one.'

'What does that mean, Maggie, ledge. . .?'

Oh. Legendary means – Oh, it was something that happened long, long ago.'

'But it was real? He was real? Was he *real*, Maggie?'

'Oh, if it happened, I expect he was.'

Doubtfully I looked at Granny. From her bed she smiled at me.

'I wish you a happy Christmas, Michael.'

'A happy Christmas, Nana.'

She beckoned me nearer. 'Come here to me.'

I felt a coin pressed in my hand.

'A little something I was saving up for the Black Babies. This time it's for you, Michael.'

I mumbled thanks.

'Look at the crib,' she said. 'Ain't it pretty?' It was on the altar near the door. 'Let you kneel down now, and say a prayer before the crib.'

'Sure I'll be going to Mass.' However I went over and knelt before the tiny figures, the ox and ass, the shepherds, Mary and Joseph and the baby figure with his little upraised arms.

Most of that day I was with Maggie and Granny, reading *Prester John*. A fowl hung roasting in front of the fire. My aunt's face was red from bending in the heat, but she was good-humoured. By the time it got dark the fowl was done. Maggie put it on a plate among the rich-smelling dark shapes on the table.

'Will I light the candle or the lamp, Mazie?' Maggie said.

'Light the candle. It's a fine big one.'

The page before me brightened.

They were all laughing and joking in the far room when I went in. Joe was wearing a red paper hat. Mother gave me a large slice of Christmas pudding.

'And what did you get from Santa, Mick?' my father said, turning round from the table.

I told him. Of course I didn't believe in Santa Claus, but it was easy

48

pretending. I'd been telling lies for years, often slipping in a guilty admission, true or false, to make the lie more convincing. I told him what toys Santa had left me. 'And Miss McCarthy gave me this.'

My father put a hand up to his face as if to say 'Excuse me'. He was only putting his cigarette in his mouth, head tilted back, half closing his eyes against the smoke. He took the book in his hands. I saw his dark-brown thumb, tobacco-stained, and the blunt, thick nail.

Joe was crouching behind the bed. He had his red paper hat on. 'Lie down!' he kept shouting at Meg. 'You're shot!' Meg refused to be shot. She left off playing with Joe and came over to show me her doll. My smallest brother, Paudeen, was gripping the edge of the table and stepping uncertainly sideways. A cup crashed from the table and he began to cry.

'Be quiet!' my mother said, fixing the kettle on the fire.

Paudeen wailed.

'Come to Daddy,' my father said. 'There, there – come to your Daddy!' He held out his arms.

'Oh, can't you whisht!' mother said to Paudeen, taking him up from the floor. 'He's only frightened. He's all right – there, there! You might cut Michael a bit of pudding, Mister. There, there. Look at that ruffian under the bed! Will you cut Meg a little bit of pudding, Mister.'

After a while I went back to Granny's room. *Prester John* was a long story. By the time I had finished it Christmas was well over.

Mister: A Dublin Childhood, 1979

THE CHRISTMAS PUDDING

J.D. Sheridan

The manuscript recipe book is always resurrected about the first week in Advent. You can make soda scones and potato cakes out of your head, it seems, but to make a plum pudding properly you must follow the rubrics.

The page opens almost of its own accord, for its fruit stains are as good as a book marker. Besides, it is the only page that is ever consulted in these degenerate days.

The making of the plum pudding is a communal activity, and in every corner of the kitchen task forces are set to work on sultanas, beef suet, mixed spices, eggs, and bread crumbs – all of which must be blended together in due course like the instruments of an orchestra, and their entries timed just as carefully. Meanwhile the conductor's head is bent over her faded and yellowing score.

My first cue is usually 'Grate bread', this being regarded as an operation which puts no great strain on the intelligence. But there is much more in it than meets the eye, and it is not by any means a matter of taking a stale loaf into a corner and worrying it. It demands care and precision, and no matter how watchful I am I always get some shredded flesh into the bowl. Meanwhile, other sub-contractors are washing currants and stoning raisins, and there isn't a word out of any of them (except when they are accusing one another to the central authority), this being one of the few occasions on which children refrain from speaking when their mouths are full.

When the stale loaf has been reduced to crusty end pieces I am seconded to the citrus fruits section and instructed to grate the rind off a lemon. This sounds easy, too, but it has its own problems, and by the time the lemon is as naked and wobbly as a soft egg from the inside of a turkey there is even less flesh on my finger tips, and I have a fellow feeling for the saints of old who were flayed alive.

However, there is a good time coming, for presently we reach the entry 'Stout or Ale', which is recipe book for 'What'll you have?' This is a man's job, and it can be entrusted only to someone of years and experience – someone who knows that you can't walk into a public house a few weeks before Christmas and ask for one miserly bottle of stout to carry away with you. The thing to do is to ask for a dozen, and it is only prudence to sample the brew whilst the man behind the counter is tying them up to look like a packet of candles.

You feel better then, and after the second bottle the cold of the glass no longer scalds the raw spots on your fingers. No fair-minded husband, however, would delay on an occasion like this. There is still much work to be done, and you must think of the little woman.

I am always a little puzzled by one line of our recipe, which reads: 'If liked, rum or whiskey may be added.' The syntax seems shaky. I like rum and whiskey, though not necessarily in that order, but I hate the thought of adding them to a sodden brown mass that looks like a cold linseed poultice, and which, in addition, has already had as much stout as it can carry. Women, however, have their own notions, and they think nothing of squandering a whole glass of brandy on an inanimate object without leaving a little in the bottom of the tumbler for consumption on the premises. This, I suggest, shows very poor consideration for a man who, if he has not worked himself to the bone, has at least given the skin off his fingers.

The plum pudding is boiled in two instalments, and when the first moiety is snoring in the pot, as if the brandy had gone to its head, a great peace descends upon the house, and the man who is paying for it all will not be thought any the worse of if he says 'I think I'll have a bottle of stout.'

The worst of Christmas is over now, and the good woman can look the neighbours in the face. For at this time of year there are two classes of women: the improvident, who 'haven't a thing done yet', and the wise matrons who have their cakes and puddings made, and lose no opportunity of saying so.

Why there should be all this fuss about plum pudding I just don't know, for it tastes no better than a bread pudding that has done a little tippling. Besides, a plum pudding is not really for eating. The family gets a tiny ration on Christmas Day, but the rest is for pride and glory, and is doled out to friends and relations, one of the ethics of Christmas being 'You can't go without tasting my pudding.'

Men visitors submit to this ritual like the heroes they are, especially if they have already got a sup out of the bottle, but their wives are enthusiastic. They say 'Oh, what a lovely pudding! I must get the recipe from you some time.' But they don't mean a word of it, for they speak before their taste buds could possibly have reached a verdict, and they are no sooner outside the door than they shrug their shoulders and add the rider: 'I didn't think much of her pudding!'

Joking Apart, 1964

CHRISTMAS EVE AT THE WHITE HART

Michael Coady

A Pheadair a aspail
a'bhfaca tú mo ghrá gheal?
Och agus ochón ó.

Man from Connemara
singing of Christ's passion
mother's pain
to shouts for mild
and bitter.

Bitter
the Christmas Eve
Kinsale was lost
Och agus ochón ó.

Christ's passion
mother's pain
rock, air, sea
of Connemara
luminous in
a labourer's song

At the White Hart
Highbury
Och agus ochón ó.

Two for a Woman, Three for a Man, 1980

THE COMMERCIALISATION OF CHRISTMAS

Anne O'Dowd and Mairead Reynolds

Christmas in the nineteenth century was influenced and changed somewhat in character by industrial developments. It is interesting to note that the family was the unit towards which the commercial promotion of Christmas was directed. By 1890 it was said: 'Now do old gentlemen buy new woollen wrappers, and young ones new kid gloves, and both of them purchase innumerable Christmas cards covered in angels and robins and holly; they also spend small fortunes in postage stamps, and feel bored with addressing so many envelopes. Now are public halls and private houses decorated with a profusion of evergreens and flags, mottoes and seasonable proverbs. Now are postmen, dustmen, lamplighters and news-boys extraordinary civil.'[1]

The new style of Christmas benefited from the development in the printing industry. The use of steam for the printing presses meant that books and other printed matter could be produced more cheaply. The first Christmas annual was probably *The Christmas Box*, a collection of poems, adventure stories and anecdotes, edited by T. Crofton Croker in 1828. Other annuals for children appeared the following year. Two Irish publications were *The Weekly Freeman's Christ-Cards* and *Christmas Chimes, A Round of Stories, Enigmas and Charades for the Christmas Fireside*. The subject matter had a more Irish flavour than in modern Irish publications.

Another result of improved printing was the Christmas card. The first such card was designed in 1843 by J.C. Horsley, R.A.[2] It was the same size as a visiting card and was printed as a lithograph and later hand-coloured. It showed alms-giving and a large prosperous family at dinner, with the legend below, 'A Merry Christmas and A Happy New Year to you'. Only about a thousand of these cards were sold.[3] The introduction, in 1840, of the new postal system meant that the charge was paid by the sender and not by the recipient. Christmas cards did not become popular until about 1870 when the cheaper rate of a halfpenny for postcards was introduced.

Throughout the nineteenth century playthings of many materials, such as wood, bone and rush, were still made in the home. By 1850 a number of Irish firms specialised in the production of fine wooden toys. Kirby's toy factory of O'Connell Street and later of Grafton Street was one of the better known firms. It was well established by 1850 and it specialised in rocking horses and toys. Another Dublin producer was E. Lawrence and Co., who exhibited Irish-manufactured toys and dolls in the Great Exhibition in London in 1851. Favourite toys of the period included cricket bats, architectural models, drums, guns, pistols, swords, tambourines as well as rocking horses. An import trade in toys also began about this time.

The newspaper advertisements for the second half of the nineteenth century show an increasing variety of toys. In 1865, Lawrence's advertised simple toys such as Parlour Croquet, Magic Lanterns, Nursery Yachts and horses on wheels. Ten years later Switzer Ferguson and Co. advertised a Windmill in motion, a Ship on a foaming sea, Tram Cars and railways, Humming Toys and Tool Chests. Twenty years later Todd Burns and Co. advertised French toys including a French clown playing a violin, a 'balancing lady who turns somersaults over a chair' and construction toys of ships and buses. All of the toys cost one shilling (5 new pence). Toys at the World's Fair Stores, 30 Henry Street, all cost 6½d (about 2½ new pence) each. This store used special displays of mechanical toys to attract customers. The display in 1895 included figures in wax, a humming bird bought at the Chicago Trade Fair and a French toy of a barber shaving a portly man who moved his head from side to side and then looked at himself in a mirror.[4]

During the nineteenth century it was expected that toys would last for generations and consequently the materials used were of the highest quality. Most of the wooden toys were made in Ireland. The best known producers were in Cushendall, County Antrim, Killarney, County Kerry, and Kirby's factory, Dublin.

French mechanical toys became increasingly sought after towards the end of the nineteenth century, but even they had to compete against cheaper German products such as rifles, sabres, helmets, regiments of tin soldiers and cannons that shot peas[5]. . . Wooden dolls, both large and small, were made in Ireland throughout the first half of the nineteenth century.

[1] The *Irish Monthly*, 1890, p.34.
[2] See Michael Harrison, *The Story of Christmas*, London, undated, c. 1954, pp.184f.
[3] George Buday, *The Story of the Christmas Card*, London, undated, c. 1952, pp.4f.
[4] The *Sunday World*, Dec. 1895, p.5.
[5] *New Ireland Review*, 30, 1909, p.301.

Christmas and the Children, 1976

THE CRIB IN THE CARMELITE CHURCH, DUBLIN

W.M. Letts

Foreninst the Crib there kneels a little child,
Behind him in her ragged shawl his mother,
For all the ages that have passed one child
    Still finds God in another.

Now, look-a how he wonders when he sees .
The shepherds with their lambs beside the manger,
The cattle, poor dumb creatures, looking down
    Upon the little Stranger.

An' there's our Saviour lying in the hay,
Behind Him in her shawl His watchful mother;
Two mothers with their sons, each knows the joys
    And sorrows of the other.

The father kneels away there by the door,
The hands he clasps in prayer are rough with labour;
The likes of him that hunger and that toil
    Once called Saint Joseph neighbour.

Outside the Church the people travel by,
The sick and sad, the needy, the neglected.
But just across the threshold Bethlehem lies,
    Where none will be rejected.

Songs from Leinster, 1923

ANOTHER CHRISTMAS

William Trevor

You always looked back, she thought. You looked back at other years, other Christmas cards arriving, the children younger. There was the year Patrick had cried, disliking the holly she was decorating the living-room with. There was the year Bridget had got a speck of coke in her eye on Christmas Eve and had to be taken to the hospital at Hammersmith in the middle of the night. There was the first year of their marriage, when she and Dermot were still in Waterford. And ever since they'd come to London there was the presence on Christmas Day of their landlord, Mr Joyce, a man whom they had watched becoming elderly.

She was middle-aged now, with touches of grey in her fluffy jet-black hair, a woman known for her cheerfulness, running a bit to fat. Her husband was the opposite: thin and seeming ascetic, with more than a hint of the priest in him, a good man. 'Will we get married, Norah?' he'd said one night in the Tara Ballroom in Waterford, November 6, 1953. The proposal had astonished her: it was his brother Ned, bulky and fresh-faced, a different kettle of fish altogether, whom she'd been expecting to make it.

Patiently he held a chair for her while she strung paper-chains across the room, from one picture-rail to another. He warned her to be careful about attaching anything to the electric light. He still held the chair while she put sprigs of holly behind the pictures. He was cautious by nature and alarmed by little things, particularly anxious in case she fell off chairs. He'd never mount a chair himself, to put up decorations or anything else: he'd be useless at it in his opinion, and it was his opinion that mattered. He'd never been able to do a thing about the house but it didn't matter because since the boys had grown up they'd attended to whatever she couldn't manage herself. You wouldn't dream of re-marking on it: he was the way he was, considerate and thoughtful in what he did do, teetotal, clever, full of fondness for herself and for the family they'd reared, full of respect for her also.

'Isn't it remarkable how quick it comes round, Norah?' he said while he held the chair. 'Isn't it no time since last year?'

'No time at all.'

'Though a lot happened in the year, Norah.'

'An awful lot happened.'

Two of the pictures she decorated were scenes of Waterford: the quays and a man driving sheep past the Bank of Ireland. Her mother had given them to her, taking them down from the hall of the farmhouse.

There was a picture of the Virgin and Child, and other, smaller pictures. She placed her last sprig of holly, a piece with berries on it, above the Virgin's halo.

'I'll make a cup of tea,' she said, descending from the chair and smiling at him.

'A cup of tea'd be great, Norah.'

The living-room, containing three brown armchairs and a table with upright chairs around it, and a sideboard with a television set on it, was crowded by this furniture and seemed even smaller than it was because of the decorations that had been added. On the mantelpiece, above a built-in gas fire, Christmas cards were arrayed on either side of an ornate green clock.

The house was in a terrace in Fulham. It had always been too small for the family, but now that Patrick and Brendan no longer lived there things were easier. Patrick had married a girl called Pearl six months ago, almost as soon as his period of training with the Midland Bank had ended. Brendan was training in Liverpool, with a firm of computer manufacturers. The three remaining children were still at school, Bridget at the nearby convent, Cathal and Tom at the Sacred Heart Primary. When Patrick and Brendan had moved out the room they'd always shared had become Bridget's. Until then Bridget had slept in her parents' room and she'd have to return there this Christmas because Brendan would be back for three nights. Patrick and Pearl would just come for Christmas Day. They'd be going to Pearl's people, in Croydon, on Boxing Day – St Stephen's Day, as Norah and Dermot always called it, in the Irish manner.

'It'll be great, having them all,' he said. 'A family again, Norah.'

'And Pearl.'

'She's part of us now, Norah.'

'Will you have biscuits with your tea? I have a packet of Nice.'

He said he would, thanking her. He was a meter-reader with North Thames Gas, a position he had held for twenty-one years, ever since he'd emigrated. In Waterford he'd worked as a clerk in the Customs, not earning very much and not much caring for the stuffy, smoke-laden office he shared with half-a-dozen other clerks. He had come to England because Norah had thought it was a good idea, because she'd always wanted to work in a London shop. She'd been given a job in Dickins & Jones, in the household linens department, and he'd been taken on as a meter-reader, cycling from door to door, remembering the different houses and where the meters were situated in each, being agreeable to householders: all of it suited him from the start. He devoted time to thought while he rode about, and in particular to religious matters.

In her small kitchen she made the tea and carried it on a tray into the living-room. She'd been late this year with the decorations. She always liked to get them up a week in advance because they set the mood, making everyone feel right for Christmas. She'd been busy with stuff for a stall Father Malley had asked her to run for his Christmas Sale. A fashion stall he'd called it, but not quite knowing what he meant she'd just asked people for any old clothes they had, jumble really. Because of the time it had taken she hadn't had a minute to see to the decorations until this afternoon, two days before Christmas Eve. But that, as it turned out, had been all for the best. Bridget and Cathal and Tom had gone up to Putney to the pictures, Dermot didn't work on a Monday afternoon: it was convenient that they'd have an hour or two alone together because there was the matter of Mr Joyce to bring up. Not that she wanted to bring it up, but it couldn't be just left there.

'The cup that cheers,' he said, breaking a biscuit in half. Deliberately she put off raising the subject she had in mind. She watched him nibbling the biscuit and then dropping three heaped spoons of sugar into his tea and stirring it. He loved tea. The first time he'd taken her out, to the Savoy Cinema in Waterford, they'd had tea afterwards in the cinema café and they'd talked about the film and about people they knew. He'd come to live in Waterford from the country, from the farm his brother had inherited, quite close to her father's farm. He reckoned he'd settled, he told her that night: Waterford wasn't sensational, but it suited him in a lot of ways. If he hadn't married her he'd still be there, working eight hours a day in the Customs and not caring for it, yet managing to get by because he had his religion to assist him.

'Did we get a card from Father Jack yet?' he inquired, referring to a distant cousin, a priest in Chicago.

'Not yet. But it's always on the late side, Father Jack's. It was February last year.'

She sipped her tea, sitting in one of the other brown armchairs, on the other side of the gas fire. It was pleasant being there alone with him in the decorated room, the green clock ticking on the mantelpiece, the Christmas cards, dusk gathering outside. She smiled and laughed, taking another biscuit while he lit a cigarette. 'Isn't this great?' she said. 'A bit of peace for ourselves?'

Solemnly he nodded.

'Peace comes dropping slow,' he said, and she knew he was quoting from some book or other. Quite often he said things she didn't understand. 'Peace and goodwill,' he added, and she understood that all right.

He tapped the ash from his cigarette into an ashtray which was kept for his use, beside the gas fire. All his movements were slow. He was a slow thinker, even though he was clever. He arrived at a conclusion, having thought long and carefully; he balanced everything in his mind. 'We must think about that, Norah,' he said that day, twenty-two years ago, when she'd suggested that they should move to England. A week later he'd said that if she really wanted to he'd agree.

They talked about Bridget and Cathal and Tom. When they came in from the cinema they'd only just have time to change their clothes before setting out again for the Christmas party at Bridget's convent.

'It's a big day for them. Let them lie in in the morning, Norah.'

'They could lie in for ever,' she said, laughing in case there might seem to be harshness in this recommendation. With Christmas excitement running high, the less she heard from them the better.

'Did you get Cathal the gadgets he wanted?'

'Chemistry stuff. A set in a box.'

'You're great the way you manage, Norah.'

She denied that. She poured more tea for both of them. She said, as casually as she could:

'Mr Joyce won't come. I'm not counting him in for Christmas Day.'

'He hasn't failed us yet, Norah.'

'He won't come this year.' She smiled through the gloom at him. 'I think we'd best warn the children about it.'

'Where would he go if he didn't come here? Where'd he get his dinner?'

'Lyons used to be open in the old days.'

'He'd never do that.'

'The Bulrush Café has a turkey dinner advertised. There's a lot of people go in for that now. If you have a mother doing a job she maybe hasn't the time for the cooking. They go out to a hotel or a café, three or four pounds a head –'

'Mr Joyce wouldn't go to a café. No one could go into a café on their own on Christmas Day.'

'He won't come here, dear.'

It had to be said: it was no good just pretending, laying a place for the old man on an assumption that had no basis to it. Mr Joyce would not come because Mr Joyce, last August, had ceased to visit them. Every Friday night he used to come, for a cup of tea and a chat, to watch the nine o'clock news with them. Every Christmas Day he'd brought carefully chosen presents for the children, and chocolates and nuts and cigarettes. He'd given Patrick and Pearl a radio as a wedding present.

'I think he'll come all right. I think maybe he hasn't been too well. God help him, it's a great age, Norah.'

'He hasn't been ill, Dermot.'

Every Friday Mr Joyce had sat there in the third of the brown armchairs, watching the television, his bald head inclined so that his good ear was closer to the screen. He was tallish, rather bent now, frail and bony, with a modest white moustache. In his time he'd been a builder, which was how he had come to own property in Fulham, a self-made man who'd never married. That evening in August he had been quite as usual. Bridget had kissed him goodnight because for as long as she could remember she'd always done that when he came on Friday evenings. He'd asked Cathal how he was getting on with his afternoon paper round.

There had never been any difficulties over the house. They considered that he was fair in his dealings with them; they were his tenants and his friends. When the Irish bombed English people to death in Birmingham and Guildford he did not cease to arrive every Friday evening and on Christmas Day. The bombings were discussed after the News, the Tower of London bomb, the bomb in the bus, and all the others. 'Maniacs,' Mr Joyce said and nobody contradicted him.

'He would never forget the children, Norah. Not at Christmastime.'

His voice addressed her from the shadows. She felt the warmth of the gas fire reflected in her face and knew if she looked in a mirror she'd see that she was quite flushed. Dermot's face never reddened. Even though he was nervy, he never displayed emotion. On all occasions his face retained its paleness, his eyes acquired no glimmer of passion. No wife could have a better husband, yet in the matter of Mr Joyce he was so wrong it almost frightened her.

'Is it tomorrow I call in for the turkey?' he said.

She nodded, hoping he'd ask her if anything was the matter because as a rule she never just nodded in reply to a question. But he didn't say anything. He stubbed his cigarette out. He asked if there was another cup of tea in the pot.

'Dermot, would you take something round to Mr Joyce?'

'A message, is it?'

'I have a tartan tie for him.'

'Wouldn't you give it to him on the day, Norah? Like you always do.' He spoke softly, still insisting. She shook her head.

It was all her fault. If she hadn't said they should go to England, if she hadn't wanted to work in a London shop, they wouldn't be caught in the trap they'd made for themselves. Their children spoke with London accents. Patrick and Brendan worked for English firms and would make their homes in England. Patrick had married an English girl. They were Catholics and they had Irish names, yet home for them was not Waterford.

'Could you make it up with Mr Joyce, Dermot? Could you go round with the tie and say you were sorry?'

'Sorry?'

'You know what I mean.' In spite of herself her voice had acquired a trace of impatience, an edginess that was unusual in it. She did not ever speak to him like that. It was the way she occasionally spoke to the children.

'What would I say I was sorry for, Norah?'

61

'For what you said that night.' She smiled, calming her agitation. He lit another cigarette, the flame of the match briefly illuminating his face. Nothing had changed in his face. He said:

'I don't think Mr Joyce and I had any disagreement, Norah.'

'I know, Dermot. You didn't mean anything –'

'There was no disagreement, girl.'

There had been no disagreement, but on that evening in August something else had happened. On the nine o'clock news there had been a report of another outrage and afterwards, when Dermot had turned the television off, there'd been the familiar comment on it. He couldn't understand the mentality of people like that, Mr Joyce said yet again, killing just anyone, destroying life for no reason. Dermot had shaken his head over it, she herself had said it was uncivilised. Then Dermot had added that they mustn't of course forget what the Catholics in the North had suffered. The bombs were a crime but it didn't do to forget that the crime would not be there if generations of Catholics in the North had not been treated as animals. There'd been a silence then, a difficult kind of silence which she'd broken herself. All that was in the past, she'd said hastily, in a rush, nothing in the past or the present or anywhere else could justify the killing of innocent people. Even so, Dermot had added, it didn't do to avoid the truth. Mr Joyce had not said anything.

'I'd say there was no need to go round with the tie, Norah. I'd say he'd make the effort on Christmas Day.'

'Of course he won't.' Her voice was raised, with more than impatience in it now. But her anger was controlled. 'Of course he won't come.'

'It's a time for goodwill, Norah. Another Christmas: to remind us.'

He spoke slowly, the words prompted by some interpretation of God's voice in answer to a prayer. She recognised that in his deliberate tone.

'It isn't just another Christmas. It's an awful kind of Christmas. It's a Christmas to be ashamed, and you're making it worse, Dermot.' Her lips were trembling in a way that was uncomfortable. If she tried to calm herself she'd become jittery instead, she might even begin to cry. Mr Joyce had been generous and tactful, she said loudly. It made no difference to Mr Joyce that they were Irish people, that their children went to school with the children of IRA men. Yet his generosity and his tact had been thrown back in his face. Everyone knew that the Catholics in the North had suffered, that generations of injustice had been twisted into the shape of a cause. But you couldn't say it to an old man who had hardly been outside Fulham in his life. You couldn't say it because when you did it sounded like an excuse for murder.

'You have to state the truth, Norah. It's there to be told.'

'I never yet cared for a North of Ireland person, Catholic or Protestant.

62

Let them fight it out and not bother us.'

'You shouldn't say that, Norah.'

'It's more of your truth for you.'

He didn't reply. There was the gleam of his face for a moment as he drew on his cigarette. In all their married life they had never had a quarrel that was in any way serious, yet she felt herself now in the presence of a seriousness that was too much for her. She had told him that whenever a new bombing took place she prayed it might be the work of the Angry Brigade, or any group that wasn't Irish. She'd told him that in shops she'd begun to feel embarrassed because of her Waterford accent. He'd said she must have courage, and she realised now that he had drawn on courage himself when he'd made the remark to Mr Joyce. He would have prayed and considered before making it. He would have seen it in the end as his Catholic duty.

'He thinks you don't condemn people being killed.' She spoke quietly even though she felt a wildness inside her. She felt she should be out on the streets, shouting in her Waterford accent, violently stating that the bombers were more despicable with every breath they drew, that hatred and death were all they deserved. She saw herself on Fulham Broadway, haranguing the passers-by, her greying hair blown in the wind, her voice more passionate than it had ever been before. But none of it was the kind of thing she could do because she was not that kind of woman. She hadn't the courage, any more than she had the courage to urge her anger to explode in their living-room. For all the years of her marriage there had never been the need of such courage before: she was aware of that, but found no consolation in it.

'I think he's maybe seen it by now,' he said. 'How one thing leads to another.'

She felt insulted by the words. She willed herself the strength to shout, to pour out a torrent of fury at him, but the strength did not come. Standing up, she stumbled in the gloom and felt a piece of holly under the sole of her shoe. She turned the light on.

'I'll pray that Mr Joyce will come,' he said.

She looked at him, pale and thin, with his priestly face. For the first time since he had asked her to marry him in the Tara Ballroom she did not love him. He was cleverer than she was, yet he seemed half blind. He was good, yet he seemed hard in his goodness, as though he'd be better without it. Up to the very last moment on Christmas Day there would be the pretence that their landlord might arrive, that God would answer a prayer because His truth had been honoured. She considered it hypocrisy, unable to help herself in that opinion.

He talked but she did not listen. He spoke of keeping faith with their own, of being a Catholic. Crime begot crime, he said, God wanted it to be known that one evil led to another. She continued to look at him while he spoke, pretending to listen but wondering instead if in twelve months time, when another Christmas came, he would still be cycling from house to house to read gas meters. Or would people have objected, requesting a meter-reader who was not Irish? An objection to a man with an Irish accent was down-to-earth and ordinary. It didn't belong in the same grand category as crime begetting crime or God wanting something to be known, or in the category of truth and conscience. In the present circumstances the objection would be understandable and fair. It seemed even right that it should be made, for it was a man with an Irish accent in whom the worst had been brought out by the troubles that had come, who was guilty of a cruelty no one would have believed him capable of. Their harmless elderly landlord might die in the course of that same year, a friendship he had valued lost, his last Christmas lonely. Grand though it might seem in one way, all of it was petty.

Once, as a girl, she might have cried, but her contented marriage had caused her to lose that habit. She cleared up the tea things, reflecting that the bombers would be pleased if they could note the victory they'd scored in a living-room in Fulham. And on Christmas Day, when a family sat down to a conventional meal, the victory would be greater. There would be crackers and chatter and excitement, the Queen and the Pope would deliver speeches. Dermot would discuss these Christmas messages with Patrick and Brendan, as he'd discussed them in the past with Mr Joyce. He would be as kind as ever. He would console Bridget and Cathal and Tom by saying that Mr Joyce hadn't been up to the journey. And whenever she looked at him she would remember the Christmases of the past. She would feel ashamed of him, and of herself.

Lovers of their Time and other Stories, 1978

O friend unchanging,
  Christmas has come again,
Bringing the thought of you
  Vividly into my memory.

Joy be for ever upon you
  With lasting prosperity;
And with this little card
  Take from me my blessing.

Douglas Hyde.

CHRISTMAS AT LUGGALA

Beatrice Behan

Luggala,[1] as Brendan used to say, was a house where you could say anything you liked provided you didn't take too long and were witty. On Christmas Eve he had been at his best and was still in high spirits when everyone else had gone to bed. He had a habit of wandering through the maze of winding corridors, singing, *'Adeste Fideles'* to the tune of 'The Coolin'. He was in the middle of his song when he tumbled head over heels down a flight of narrow, curving stairs leading to the servants' quarters. He lay at the bottom with his feet wedged against a door.

Sis, the housekeeper, heard his cries for help. She tried to open the door from the servants' rooms. But as she pushed mightily from her side, Brendan's feet kept jamming the door from his side. He was inextricably wedged in the cramped space between the bottom steps and the door.

Cummins[2] had a theory that if Brendan wasn't put to bed he would fall down the stairs, and it had happened. There were times when Cummins had helped him climb the stairs and placed a bathtowel under his head on the pillow lest he should throw up during the night; there was even a time when Lucien Freud had hoisted him on his shoulders and carried him to bed. But now he lay at the foot of the stairs while I slept in one of the Blue Room's two single beds, unaware of the commotion.

'For Jaysus' sake, get me out of here!' Brendan called to Sis.

'Are you all right, Mr Behan?'

'How in Jaysus' name could I be all right when I've fallen down the fucking stairs? If I was all right I wouldn't be here. Why don't you get me out?'

'I'm afraid I can't, sir. I can't open the door.'

'Well, get someone who can.'

Sis roused May, one of the housemaids, and May went running through the labyrinth of corridors, up and down stairs, until she reached the foot of the staircase where Brendan lay.

'How in God's name did you get there, Mr Behan?' she wanted to know.

Brendan kept his patience.

'I missed the light,' he said. 'I put my hand up for the switch at the top of the stairs and I missed it.'

May gripped him under both arms and heaved him into a sitting position.

'You may be a big man, Mr Behan,' she told him, 'but you're not heavy.'

Blood was oozing from a gash on his head, and when Sis was able to open the door from the other side she brought a basin of water and bathed the gash and then placed a damp towel around his head.

'It's Christmas morning isn't it?' Brendan inquired.

'That's right, Mr Behan.'

'Well, I only hope the holy Mother of God will look after you for what you've done for me.'

As dawn broke they made him tea. May brought a cup to me in the Blue Room and I noticed the other bed had not been slept in.

'Where's my husband?' I asked.

'He's had a little fall, Mrs Behan,' said May. 'But don't worry, he's not hurt bad.'

Later we helped Brendan into the Rolls, and Sam, who was the farm manager, drove us back to Dublin. Brendan lay inert in the back seat. I told him that as soon as we reached the town of Bray I intended to go to Christmas Mass.

'You can go where you bloody well like.'

Then as an afterthought he added, 'I suppose I might as well go too.'

His white shirt was grubby and open to his navel and his chest and face were spattered with blood. People turned to stare at us in the church. But I pretended not to notice them.

When Mass was over we bundled him back into the Rolls. I decided to visit friends of mine who might provide us with Christmas lunch, for there was no food in our house, not even a loaf of bread.

Brendan disagreed. 'We're going to my friend's,' he said. 'Sam, take us to Bill Finnegan's.'

Bill Finnegan was a taxi-driver who had been a barber. If he and his wife were surprised to see a Rolls draw up outside their small house in Inchicore, they did not show it.

'This is my friend, Sam,' Brendan told them. 'He'll have a drink.'

I could see Sam was impatient to return to Luggala, so I asked Brendan where he intended to spend the evening.

'Crumlin,' he said, which was where his parents lived.

Sam drove through gloomy streets lined with Corporation houses until he found Kildare Road.

'Sam,' invited Brendan, 'come and have some Christmas dinner.'

Someone produced two slices of bread with a piece of chicken between them and a large mug of tea. Sam ate the food dutifully and then said, 'I must be getting back now, Mr Behan.'

'You're not going yet,' Brendan protested. 'We have more calls to make.'

'Sam must get back to Luggala,' I told my husband. And with that

Sam and the Rolls were gone.

I sat in the Behan living room in the bosom of my in-laws. This was the family I had chosen to join when I married Brendan Behan in what had been described as the most unlikely union in Ireland. And of that family Brendan was the most remarkable member.

NOTES

[1] The eighteenth-century country house of Lady Oonagh, of the Guinness family.
[2] The butler.

Brendan Behan: Interviews and Recollections, Volume 2
(edited by E.H. Mikhail, 1984)

CHRISTMAS IN BELFAST, 1940

Brian Moore

Mrs Burke made an excellent trifle which was always served on Christmas Day as a first pudding. So, when old Mary entered the dining room, holding aloft the plum pudding ringed by brandy flames and decorated with a sprig of holly, there were groans of mock protest from the family and guests. Canon Wood patted the convexity of his black waistcoat, shut his eyes, and shook his head slowly from side to side. Mrs Sullivan, a widow, who had been a bridesmaid at Gavin's parents' wedding, said that only on Christmas Day and in this house did she believe she committed the sin of gluttony. However, Mrs Burke, Gavin, Kathy, and Owen, knowing how easily old Mary was offended if one did not eat her puddings, politely nibbled on small portions. Mr Burke declined. A few minutes later, when the ladies had retired to the up-stairs sitting room, he broke the seal on a box of cigars and, going to the sideboard, brought out a decanter of port.

'Try this, Malachy,' he told the Canon. 'And, in honor of Christmas, I think I'll let you boys try it too.'

'Is this Tom's stuff?' the Canon asked, peering at his glass. The Canon had been to school with Gavin's father and with his Uncle Tom. Mr Burke nodded and passed around the box of cigars. 'Probably the last decent port we'll have for a long time,' the Canon decided.

'No, no,' Mr Burke said. 'This war's as good as over. In fact, I wouldn't give it another six months.'

'I wouldn't count the British out just yet, if I were you,' the Canon warned. '*Gott mit uns* is a sight more applicable to British history than ever it was to the German Reich.'

'Oh, come now,' said Mr Burke. 'The Luftwaffe's bombing the britches off them. You heard about the riots in Liverpool last week?'

The Canon had not heard a thing.

'John Sherry's wife was over, saw it with her own two eyes. People were marching around in the streets, carrying placards, asking Churchill to make peace and stop the bombings. Mounted police charged them. There was quite a panic, she says.'

'Is that so? In Liverpool. Well, well.'

'And in other places too, I'll bet,' Mr Burke said. 'Oh, the English are going to find out that their troubles are only beginning. Mark my words, Hitler won't be an easy master. He won't spare them, not after the way they turned down that perfectly reasonable peace offer he made last summer.'

'Lord knows, these bombings of women and children are sickening, no matter which side does it,' the Canon said. 'We're very lucky over here. Ah, I forgot. We have an air-raid expert, right at this table. Eh, Gavin?'

'Some expert,' Owen said. 'Never saw a bomb in his life.'

'Or will see one, please God,' the Canon said. 'That's one advantage of living in a backwater, I must say.'

'What did they do at that post of yours today.' Mr Burke asked. 'Did they have a party?'

'Sort of, but it fell flat. Craig, our leader, forbade any booze. The men were furious.'

'It must be a very tiresome job,' the Canon said, 'sitting around all the time.'

'It gives me time to study,' Gavin said, looking at his father. His father caught the look and told the Canon, 'Yes, Gavin's trying the London Matric again. I think he's decided to put his back into it this time.'

'Then he'll have no trouble passing,' the Canon said. 'There's no shortage of brains in this family. How are *you* doing, Owen?'

'Oh, Owen's doing very well,' his father said. 'I've never had any trouble with Owen. He wasn't always off to dances like some boys I could mention.'

'Well, I hope there's one dance he goes off to, very soon,' the Canon said. 'And that's the school Old Boys' Dance on New Year's Eve. I hope you'll all buy tickets for it.'

'I never go to dances, Malachy, you know that,' Mr Burke said. 'But the boys will go.'

'With fair damsels, I trust,' the Canon said, winking at Owen and Gavin.

'Like Sally Shannon?' Owen said to Gavin.

'And the beauteous Miss Cooke for you?' Gavin asked.

'She'll do,' Owen said.

'Excellent.' The Canon raised his glass. 'As Chairman of the Dance Committee, I'm delighted to hear that the girls will be up to snuff.'

'Did you listen to the King's speech today?' Mr Burke said.

'I had something better to do,' the Canon said, 'than listen to that idiot.'

'On the contrary,' Mr Burke said. 'I wouldn't miss it for anything. He's great value. What an orator. They must be sitting on eggs at Windsor Castle, waiting for him to trip up.'

'Ah, poor devil,' the Canon said. 'What can he say, even if he's fit to say it? It's been all bad tidings this last year. The only hope for them now is if the Americans come in on their side.'

'Too late', Mr Burke declared. 'Wasn't that what somebody said in a speech in the Commons last spring? "It's always too little or too late, or both, that's the road to disaster." No, Malachy, I'd not give them another six months. Bet you a pound.'

   'A pound,' the Canon said. 'All right. Imagine *me* betting on England.'

The Emperor of Ice Cream, 1966

THE MAGI

Michael Walsh

Of all the dawn-flushed mornings of the earth
That lit the east throughout your space of days
Was none like this. . .

For you were travellers on
The highest Quest of all; no dreamers lured
By fabled lands within the setting sun
Nor lost Atlantis where the sky is low. . .

What thoughts were yours, Kings riding in the dawn
When God gave to your morn another star!

Red on the Holly

UNCERTAIN PLANS FOR CHRISTMAS

Michael Collins

23 December 1921

My dearest Kit,

The wee note which accompanies this was written yesterday morning but the day came so strenuous that I was unable to finish it. You'd scarcely credit a thing like that, would you? Today is, however, somewhat of a free day – alas! free only from the routine of a debate – and I must try to do some shopping. What shall I get you? I must get it today as I may have to go to Cork by the night train tonight. My plans are still uncertain for Xmas (at least my personal plans) but it is practically certain that I must go to Cork. This will mean of course that I can't get down to you but I'll go down some time around New Year's day, perhaps on Friday, and I could then return on Monday, but I'll let you know this directly I return from Cork. That Donegal visit certainly looks very enticing and I am really sorry the offer could not be taken advantage of just now but it will some time D.V.

Now you may not hear from me again until I do return – it is possibly no use writing as the delays would be terrible. However I may send a wire. Am rushing away now to see A.G.* Bye Bye. Best of times for Xmas. Don't overeat yourself! Please give them all my regards. With all my very fondest love to you and many a special thought and wish at this time.

Yours,
M.

You needn't have been so quick with that £15. Why didn't you keep it? Love again.
M.

NOTE
*Arthur Griffith

In Great Haste: the Letters of Michael Collins and Kitty Kiernan, 1983

CHRISTMAS EVE

John Hewitt

NOTE IN PRELUDE

There is a time for the crying thin,
the lyric tone of the violin.
There is a time for the hammered song
of the cane-bang'd drum and the brasslunged gong.

THE SONG

At ten o'clock on Christmas Eve
I thanked my host and took my leave,
and shut the door, and hurried down
the lane that leads to the little town.

Snow fell lightly, with never a noise,
making the houses look like toys:
the windows shining like coloured paper
that one holds up before a taper.
When snow lay inches, inches thick,
and steelshod heels made now no click,
the wind came up and cleared the sky
with a gusty broom and a huswife's eye.
The stars were shining knockers bright
across the great halldoor of Night.
The trees in the fields stood still as stone:
a far dog barked alone. . . alone. . .

At Crowcopse Manor the old church clock
crashed at the half and wakened a cock.
At Deadman's Hollow my watch-face showed
eleven o'clock. . . and half the road.
At a quarter to twelve I heard a sound,
it rang in the air and all around.
Between two stars that sang and shone
an angel trumpeted a mellow tone.
Behind him far, and behind the stars,
seraphs ran in their flaming cars:
and silver wings and glowing feet
glittered along the golden street,
and golden voices and golden lutes

74

and dulcimers and golden flutes,
O high skycrying violins
woke the Coda that begins
with golden instruments, golden throats,
and deep earthshaking organ notes. . .

This Christmas morn
to you is born
a Christ again.
Rejoice, O men!

Then I saw the Mother sitting on the Throne,
and a little laughing baby that held her as his own.
Then I saw the Stable, and the sherpherds kneeling there,
and old bewildered Joseph with the starlight in his hair,
and the cattle in the corner, and the crib among the hay,
and the droopeared little donkey with the melancholy bray.
But when I heard that sudden bray
the vision vanished clean away:
and heaven shut; and the music died,
and I stood alone on the white hillside.

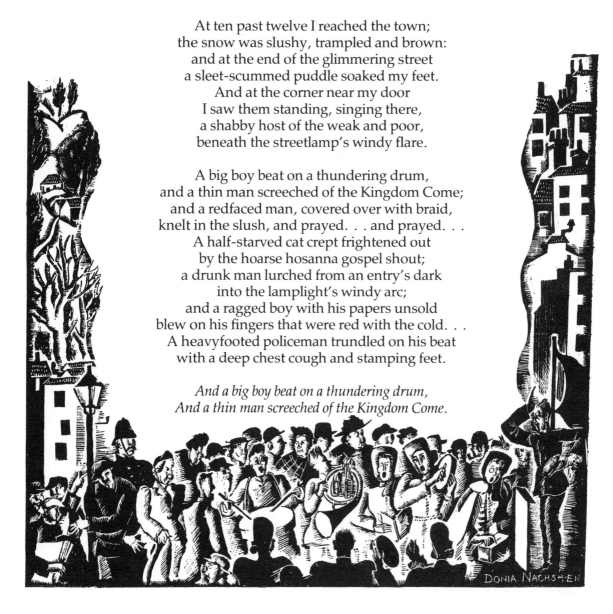

At ten past twelve I reached the town;
the snow was slushy, trampled and brown:
and at the end of the glimmering street
a sleet-scummed puddle soaked my feet.
And at the corner near my door
I saw them standing, singing there,
a shabby host of the weak and poor,
beneath the streetlamp's windy flare.

A big boy beat on a thundering drum,
and a thin man screeched of the Kingdom Come;
and a redfaced man, covered over with braid,
knelt in the slush, and prayed. . . and prayed. . .
A half-starved cat crept frightened out
by the hoarse hosanna gospel shout;
a drunk man lurched from an entry's dark
into the lamplight's windy arc;
and a ragged boy with his papers unsold
blew on his fingers that were red with the cold. . .
A heavyfooted policeman trundled on his beat
with a deep chest cough and stamping feet.

And a big boy beat on a thundering drum,
And a thin man screeched of the Kingdom Come.

Radio Times, December 18, 1931

'NOTHING ON'

Eamon Kelly

Though it might not seem so, television and radio planners go to quite extreme lengths to delight and entertain their respective publics on Christmas Day. Many years ago, through some oversight, I was included in Radio Eireann's bumper Christmas billing. As the programme was pre-recorded before a live (ha!) audience I was permitted my liberty on the day and went for a long morning walk.

On the road between Coolock and Howth I came across an itinerant tent, alone and forlorn in a wet field. As I passed it, like chickens from under a hen's wing, two children poked their heads from its flap. They were hungry: 'Mister, will the shops be open soon?'

'Not today,' I told them, 'nor tomorrow.' They nearly cried.

I made up my sentimental mind there and then. Tonight I would bring something to the tent for the children and a few bottles of stout for the parents. Back home I cut slices of everything that was going and packed them in a cardboard box. Our eldest – he was about four at the time – volunteered to help. We set out and would not have found the tent in the darkness if they hadn't had their radio on.

'Dad,' said our eldest, 'that's you!' The Christmas special was going out to the nation! The boy – an ardent fan of mine – was extremely pleased and proud.

We entered. The head of the family – out of courtesy – turned off the radio. They were delighted with the hamper: the children dressed up in the bright paper hats and tucked into the Christmas fare. Moving to go, and I must confess in the hope that the man would turn on the radio – that I might have an opportunity to modestly reveal my identity – I remarked: 'You needn't have turned off the radio.'

'Ah,' he shrugged, 'it's all right, there was nothing on.'

The Humour is on Me, 1980

HARD TIMES

John O'Donoghue

When Christmas Eve came we all got busy putting up the decorations. We nailed coloured pictures on the walls containing mottoes such as 'God bless all here', and 'What is home without a mother?' The O'Gradys told us where to buy them for they were far better up in the world than we were. I brought in two big turnips and cut away the tops and bottoms so that they might rest like bowls on the table. Making a hole in the top of each I fitted the ends of the great Christmas candles into them. Moll Tim was after giving them to my mother as part of her Christmas box, for we bought the groceries from her. Eileen surrounded the lower part of the candles with bunches of holly and laurel, pushing the ends into the turnips to keep the branches in position. Herself and my younger sister Abbey put coloured papers around the turnips to hide them. They also hung streamers over the holly and laurel as well as on the windows and mantelshelf.

Darkness was now falling, but the bright turf fire, built in front of a big block of ash, made the hearth look cheerful. This particular piece of wood was called the *bluck nullog*. A pot of boiled ling rested in the corner. This was a favourite Christmas Eve dish. A pot of potatoes hung over the fire and when they were boiled we all sat down for dinner in the twilight.

When it was dark my sister Abbey lit the candles, putting one on the window-sill of the room and another in the kitchen. This is always done according to an ancient custom so that wandering people can see that they are welcome and need not sleep in stables or other outhouses as the Holy Family had to do in Bethlehem long ago. My sisters and brothers went out with me to look at all the bright lights that shone around the valley. It was a lovely sight to see. The windows of distant houses shone like stars among the dark mountains. There was one light missing, however. We had always seen it from the back door on every previous Christmas. But poor Bess O'Mahoney who put it in the window was there no more to do it. She was dead, alas, the Lord have mercy on her soul, and all her family had gone to America. The house was shut now and darkness lay around it. The world would indeed be lonely if all the stars went out.

After returning to the house we sat around the fire and started talking. The *bluck nullog* burned brightly and there was a cheerful look about the kitchen.

'Well,' said my mother, looking around her, 'I hope we'll all be together this time twelve months.'

'I hope so,' said my father with a sigh, 'for lots of things can happen in a year.'

The dog began to bark outside. We listened, and after a little while we heard the tramping of nailed boots on the cobblestones of the yard. The latch was lifted and the door opened. Stephen O'Falvey and his cousin Shaun came in. They were both close relatives of ours that lived beyond Shronerue.

'A merry Christmas to all here,' said Stephen.

'The same to you, and a good many of them,' said my father, pushing back his chair. 'Welcome here. Let ye shove up to the fire.'

'We won't,' said Stephen, making himself comfortable on the settle, giving his grey frieze trousers a tug at the knees and turning down the pads at the ankles. 'There's no cold, and the world is hot enough for me indeed for I went near being burned alive this evening,' and he showed us where his waistcoat pocket was burnt by his lighted pipe put in there in a hurry by mistake.

'Look at that for you now,' said my mother with a good-humoured laugh. 'The craze for the weed will do more, I'm telling you, for the men and their pipes are a scald. Some of them would smoke the leg off a skillet, and 'tis no wonder we have accidents, by the same token.'

'Don't be so hard with us, Annie,' said Shaun, who was an easy-going man, though fond of a drop of drink, often coming home bare-headed after losing his hat, and singing at the top of his voice: 'This is the rocky road; this is the road to Dublin.'

'Were ye over at the village?' asked my father.

'We were then,' said Stephen, leaning back on the settle, 'and a little further too. Shaun and myself went down to Glenflesk to look at a few cattle we were thinking of buying from Johnnie O'Connell of The Railway Gate, but we didn't make the deal after all.'

'Johnnie took us west the road and we had a couple of drinks together,' said Shaun. 'That's what delayed us so much.'

'Where did ye get the drink around there, eroo?' asked my mother, who rarely travelled in that direction.

'Near the Gate then,' said Shaun. 'Down at Mhainus Moynihan's of Corrigeenareenka.'

'I know,' said my mother. 'I often heard Pat Mulloy say it was at a pattern on the rock there his uncle Den first met his wife and she put the "Come hither" on him.'

'There's no fear that will happen to Pat,' said my father. 'Was there any news in the village when ye came back?'

'Wisha, no then,' said Stephen. 'Nothing worth mentioning only everyone complaining about the hard times as usual.'

My mother began to lay the table, and when the visitors saw her do so they stood up to go.

'Damn it, men,' said my father, 'let ye wait and drink the tea with us.'

'The devil carry the tea we'll have then,' said Shaun, 'for our own will be waiting for us at home.'

As they moved towards the door my father stopped them, took a bottle of whiskey from behind a dish on the dresser and poured out a glass for each. Then they sat down again without much force.

'A merry Christmas to you all,' said Stephen, lifting up his glass and tilting it towards his mouth.

'The same to you both,' said my father, 'and a happy New Year as well. God help us, there is no Christmas these late years compared with what used to be. The times are too bad. People can hardly buy food not to mind drink.'

'The shopkeepers at Gurthagreenane would frighten the life out of you talking about the poverty of the country,' said my mother. 'Not a penny coming in to them from one end of the year to the other.'

'The times will be worse too,' said Shaun, finishing off his glass, 'if we don't get a change of government.'

'Yerra, changes like that make little difference,' said Stephen. 'One party is as bad as another, and they're all trying to butter their own bread first before thinking about the rest of the people. "You shouldn't bother your head about who's in or out, my good man," said Daniel O'Connell to the quarry-man making an inquiry after an election long ago. "You'll still have to go on breaking stones in any case."'

In Kerry Long Ago, 1960

AN ENGLISH CHRISTMAS, 1798

Thomas Flanagan

In the weeks and months after our deliverance from captivity, I was made aware of how deep had been the distress of my beloved Eliza. In our months of danger and anxiety, she was my certain source of strength, the firm rock of my existence. I have perhaps been remiss not to have incorporated into my narrative instances of her many acts of kindness, the example of Christian fortitude which she placed before those who shared our imprisonment. She has no gift for memorable phrase, has much humour but little of what the world terms wit. And yet, the dangers past, she communicated to me her troubled spirit, not in words, but by a manner too subdued, a distracted air. More than once I came upon her at the drawing-room windows, seated, looking out fixedly upon the narrow, empty street. And I would know that she was remembering that street filled with shouting men, remembering that men had died most horribly beneath those windows.

Accordingly, I resolved, with a swiftness seldom granted to me, that we should spend the Christmas season in Derbyshire, at the home of my brother Nicholas. We had spent in that house the first Christmas of our

81

life together, and she holds it in much affection. I knew also the power of an English Christmas as a restorative. Some there are who affect to mock it, calling it a pagan winter festival but ill-disguised, yet it has always seemed to me deeply Christian, an affirmation of the warmth of love and sympathy in the very chill of December. Eliza agreed most readily, as, to be sure, she does with all my plans and projects. I cannot recall that she has ever opposed me in anything which I have ever proposed, or disobeyed any just order which I have given. A most Christian woman.

We took the mail coach from Castlebar to Dublin, and were accompanied for part of the journey by a body of dragoons, handsome, heavy-shouldered men under the command of a young captain with a small-boned, gentle face. The coach was waiting for us outside the courthouse, a drab vehicle, unlike its splendid English counterpart, save for the shining, yellow-painted wheels. As we walked towards it, we had suddenly a glimpse into the yard, so sudden that I had no time to warn Eliza, and she looked for a moment without comprehending and then buried her face in her hands. Five forms hung from a gibbet, shapeless and black, their overcoats of tar frozen and glistening. Mr Comfort, the captain of dragoons, helped me place Eliza in the coach, and then turned to face me.

'When they hang men in this country, they make no mistake about it,' he said.

'It is horrible,' I said. 'Horrible. And in a Christian land.'

'Some question about that,' he said with a grin.

'They are Christian,' I said, 'and their souls demand the Christian burial of their bones.'

'That is Duggan there,' he said, pointing towards the form on the left end. 'I would hesitate to call that one a proper pagan, much less a Christian. In Killala –'

'I know what he did in Killala,' I said quickly.

'Of course, sir. I had forgotten. Another Killala man there, next to him. A schoolmaster. A hulking brute, was he not? Look at the size of him.'

Once he stood before me in my library, talking about *Gil Blas* and the roads of Munster. And once his voice drifted in song from the open door of the barn, where he stood among servants, his arm around a maiden's waist. An ugly sack of guts and bones, chained and tarred. I turned and climbed into the coach.

The coach rolled through the wasted country. Below us, the yellow wheels spun merrily. Dogs ran from cabins to yelp at us, and old people stood at their doors. Cattle watched us, motionless in the fields. We passed a row of burned cabins, roofless, doors like rotting mouths. Two crossroads were marked by empty gallows, maimed crosses of smooth wood, raw and weather-stained. But the land itself was wrapped in the soft Irish winter. Blue hills, distant beyond fields, the pale blue sky as wide as eternity, clouds touched with silver, quiet rivers. A world brought to perfection, marred by the violence of man.

Our Derbyshire Christmas was all that I had expected of it and more, and the greatest of my Christmas gifts was the brightness which returned to Eliza's eyes and face. All of that season's cheer was welcome to us – the Yule log, the holly, the waits who gathered outside the windows to sing, the bowls of hot, spiced wine. It was a snowy Christmas. I took many walks through a countryside which had been familiar to me from childhood – for here I had been born – but now mantled in white. No other countryside could have offered a more vivid contrast to the one which I had left. Our village was a proper village, and our inn a proper inn with its warm, snug, and well-appointed taproom.

And Nicholas is a proper English squire. He could sit for his portrait by artist or novelist, the very type of his excellent species. He has also, alas, a mind circumscribed by the boundary line of his country. If I had returned to him from a mission to Tartary, I could not have seemed a more exotic traveller. And yet he had no desire to learn from me. Rather, he wished to give me instruction, as though all of the British interest in Ireland were vested in my poor person, and he the Voice of England.

'It is intolerable, brother, intolerable that you should permit the populace of that wretched island to conspire and band together in open disloyalty and armed treason. Are there not laws, an army, militia, yeomanry? And yet you permit the island to explode.'

'I myself did not, brother,' I replied. 'I have described my parish to you. I have the care of a few hundred souls, cast away in a remote part of the island, surrounded by untold thousands of miserable wretches.'

'Untold thousands? Where? In Mayo? I don't believe you. What is the population of the island?'

'No one knows. Millions, certainly. There is much dispute upon the point.'

'Much dispute? Why should it be a matter for dispute? Mayo has its landlords, and each landlord has his tenants. Let the landlords count up the tenants, add the totals, and there you have the population. Good God!'

'No, no,' I said. 'There are tenants and subtenants and sub-subtenants and drifting men. There are mountain wastes with hundreds of Gaelic-speaking wretches clinging to the sides, and there are wretches clinging to the sides of bogs. Entire communities. Now, in winter, there are families of beggars upon every road, a pathetic spectacle. I assure you, Nicholas, it is not like England at all.'

We were seated in his library, as he chose to call a combination of office and tackroom, with a few dozen books gathering dust upon shelves. We were facing a blazing log fire, and comforting ourselves with madeira and biscuits. Nicholas's broad, sturdy legs were stretched towards the fire. He was not angry, not even very interested. It was his manner.

'Laziness,' he said. 'Laziness and Popery and treason. The curses of Ireland. The landlords are as bad as the rest of them. I've seen them in London, gambling away their rents. And I have heard them, with brogues that you would need a carving knife to cut. Expect people like that to govern properly? I don't.'

'They may not be governing much longer,' I said. 'In Dublin and London all the talk is of a union of the two kingdoms.'

'There is a fine Christmas present,' Nicholas said. 'An island swarming with beggars dropped into our lap. You were mad to take up your task there. Look at your poor wife, harried out of her wits by savages. And in the end we had to settle things for you, send over good English lads to die in your pestilent bogs. Always the same. Cromwell had to go over, and William after him. There is treason in that air; it is bred into men's bones.'

The Year of the French, 1979

TO MY DAUGHTER KATE

Daniel O'Connell

To his daughter Kate O'Connell, Aghada [Cahirciveen, Co. Kerry]

Merrion Square,
24 December 1845, Christmas Eve

My own dearest darling Catty,

Many and many a happy Christmas to my *dearest* Child, to her dear Husband and to their dearly loved girls and boy – of all of whom my heart doats.

You and I, sweet Catty, had always *a secret*, and now in strict secrecy I give you a cheque for one hundred guineas and which I send you as your Christmas box but you may, if you please, give to Charles as a new year's gift with my most affectionate love. But this must be a secret as others would *perhaps* be jealous.

I fear much that rascally politics will prevent me from seeing your darling family until summer, which will afflict my heart sorely. But God's will be done.

I mean at Easter to go to Liege to see Nell and her darlings. She is, I regret to say, in indifferent health.

I do not think Peel will be able to form a permanent ministry. We are near strange scenes, darling, favourable I do believe to poor Ireland.

What report can Charles make of the state of the potatoes in the country generally as well as his own crop.

[P.S.] *Any* Tralee or Killarney bank will cash this cheque. Pray for me all of you.

The Correspondence of Daniel O'Connell

CHRISTMAS AT HOME

C.S. Lewis

25 December 1922

We were awakened early by my father to go to the communion service. It was a dark morning with a gale blowing and some very cold rain. . . As we walked down to Church we started discussing the time of sunrise; my father saying rather absurdly that it must have risen already or it wouldn't be light. In Church it was intensely cold. Warnie offered to keep his coat on. My father expostulated and said, 'Well at least you won't keep it on when you go up to the Table.' Warnie asked why not, and was told it was 'most disrespectful.' I couldn't help wondering why. But Warnie took it off to save trouble. . . Another day exactly similar to yesterday. My father amused us by saying in a tone, almost of alarm, 'Hullo, it's stopped raining. We ought to go out,' and then adding with undisguised relief, 'Ah no, it's still raining, we needn't.' Christmas dinner, a rather deplorable ceremony, at quarter to four. Afterwards it had definitely cleared up; my father said he was too tired to go out, but encouraged Warnie and me to do so – which we did with great eagerness and set out to reach Holywood by the high road and there have a drink. It was delightful to be in the open air after so many hours confinement in one room. Fate however denied our drink; for we were met just outside Holywood by the Hamiltons' car and of course had to travel back with them. . . Early to bed, dead tired with talk and lack of ventilation. I found my mind was crumbling into the state which this place always produces; I have gone back six years to be flabby, sensual, unambitious. Headache again.

Letters of C.S. Lewis, 1966

NEAL'S MUSIC HALL IN DUBLIN,
Whereat "Messiah" was first performed.

HANDEL IN DUBLIN, 1741

Newman Flower

Handel actually finished *Messiah* on 14 September 1741. On 29 September he completed the first part of another oratorio, *Samson*, from a *libretto* which Newburgh Hamilton had based upon Milton's 'Samson Agonistes'. Yet he did not complete it until October of the following year. Music – and music that was on a scale of grandeur not often attained – was rushing from him like a flood.

He had no thought for production. The work as it was completed was put away. *Messiah* went into a drawer for seven weeks. It is doubtful if he ever intended to produce it in London, for the sickening experiences of the last few years had decided him to leave town at the first opportunity. Had an invitation not come to him in the autumn from the Lord Lieutenant of Ireland, and the Governors of the three charitable institutions in Dublin, to go to the city, it is not improbable that he might have returned to Germany, if only for a period. In which case *Messiah* would never have been first produced within the realm of the King.

The mood that was upon Handel responded immediately to the call from Dublin. If London no longer wanted him, he was at least a prophet not without honour elsewhere. Moreover, the principal charity for which his services were sought was the Mercers' Hospital in Stephen Street, which looked after the wretched prisoners in the debtors' prison – prisoners who were either fed by charity or left to starve. The fact that he had nearly been thrown into a debtors' prison so shortly before may

87

have had some influence on a great soul to which charity never appealed in vain.

He left London at the beginning of November, and broke the journey for some days at the 'Golden Falcon' at Chester, where he held private rehearsals with the company he had taken with him. Not till the 18th did he reach Dublin, for heavy seas were running in the Channel, and all the packets were late. The Irish press acclaimed him. *Faulkner's Journal*, the news-sheet of the day, announced that 'the celebrated Dr Handell' had arrived by the packet-boat from Holyhead, with an insistence on the 'Dr' which must have reminded Handel – if he saw the paper – of the Oxford exploit, and the Oxford professors who wanted his hundred pounds!

His principal singers began to reach him one by one. Mrs Cibber, who had renounced her acting at Drury Lane and her continuous playing of 'Polly' in *The Beggar's Opera*, had joined him, more to escape from a worrying husband than for the joys of an Irish *début*. One can imagine how she and Handel had hatched out the scheme in the Cibber drawing room, with Handel at the music-stool.

Mrs Cibber is supposed to have been in Dublin at the time of Handel's arrival, but on this point authorities differ. Signora Avolio arrived in a yacht soon after Handel. Handel's company was now complete. He took a house in Abbey Street and set about his affairs. William Neal, a music-publisher, had built a new music-hall in Fishamble Street, and opened it but a few weeks previously, and as Secretary of the Charities' Commission that summoned Handel from his seclusion, he placed the building at the disposal of the master.

A fierce joy in life began to surge in a flood through Handel. A rosy tinge crept across the world as he knew it. The whole social life of Dublin was shaken up by his coming. People peered through the Abbey Street windows and swore that they had seen him composing a vast and new work, which was to be a gift to the Irish nation. They called upon him at all and every hour, only to be told that Mr Handel was busy. Composing, of course. One veteran declared till the grave claimed him that he had actually seen the master composing *Messiah* at Abbey Street. Happy fellow! He carried a dream in which he truly believed through the rest of his years.

Events followed each other in rapid succession in Dublin. Mrs Cibber was flown as a sort of kite. She appeared in a play at the Theatre Royal called *The Conscious Lovers* to test out the attitude of the Irish towards the invaders. She captured the people; they thronged her carriage, smothered her with flowers. What can her success have meant to Handel? Some winnowed recollections of the days when he hustled up the Haymarket cursing wholesomely the little girl, Susanna Arne, who was drawing the crowds to the stolen version of his *Acis and Galatea*. Susanna Arne – Mrs Cibber – the prophetess of the new day. What a whirligig was life! London caught the echo of her triumph a few weeks later, and the *Gentleman's Magazine* appeared with a laudatory poem about her Dublin acting. The stars were set in their courses. Yesterday was forgotten. The hurt, the struggle had been no more than the blemish of an hour.

Handel opened his season with a performance of *L'Allegro* two days before Christmas. The piece which had failed in London was acclaimed in Dublin. 'Without Vanity,' Handel wrote to Jennens, 'the Performance was received with general Approbation.' The moral effect of this success was soon evident in him; it proved that his work had failed in London, not because of its quality. These crowding Irish people, the insistence of the Duke of Devonshire that he should repeat the performance, the inquisitive populace that hailed him as a god of music when London had forgotten him through sheer surfeit of the beauty he had given it, stirred him, excited him.

The old despairs departed. Never had he known such ecstasies at the organ. The whole spirit of the man was uprising as a root may yield new and freshened life after the surge of winter. 'The music sounds delightfully in this charming Room,' he wrote of Neal's music-hall to Jennens just before the New Year, 'which puts me in such excellent Spirits (and my health being so good) that I exert myself on the Organ with more than usual success.' The tide had begun to run again. Not for many years had Handel loved his life so much.

He followed *L'Allegro* with *Alexander's Feast*, and, after a temporary delay, caused by the illness of Mrs Cibber, he revived *Imeneo*. There was no break in the crowds. *Imeneo*, which had run its two nights to poor houses in London, was hailed now in Dublin as a triumph. So great, indeed, was the number of people seeking admission that Handel had to issue an apology through the press because he had had to turn away all members of the public who had not purchased subscribers' tickets for the season.

It was not until March 1742 that any announcement was made regarding *Messiah*.

George Frideric Handel, 1923

RYAN-

YULETIDE IN CAGE FIVE

Bobby Devlin

Christmas Eve 1973 approached and still the rain came down. We planned to have a party that night. Jehovah did not forsake us that Christmas Eve because a miracle happened in Cage Five. Our urns of milk which had been empty and left outside before the Brit raid, now bore an alcoholic beverage which tasted not of this earth. It was a repeat of the wedding feast at Canaan when Our Lord changed the jars of water into wine. If it wasn't a miracle then how the devil did it get there?

A party was held that night in our hut, and I can remember just a little of the proceedings. The goodies which our families had sent us were laid out on the tables, and it was quite an impressive spread. We couldn't wait to get at the 'Heavenly Brew'. I've never tasted anything like that before or since. I remember drinking a mug full and having to endure Hannibal's jokes when Junior Parker sang 'My Way'. We freed our native land in song, and wished our families the season's goodwill. I proposed a toast to Willie Whitelaw and we all came to the opinion that he was a big bastard.

The scene was almost Dickensian. There we all were, a right bunch of 'Tiny Tims' forgotten by old Ebeneezer Whitelaw Scrooge on Christmas Eve. The Ghosts of Christmas Past, Present or Future would not visit 'Willie Scrooge' in dread of a detention order being signed on them. At the time we were a bit harsh on Willie, because Francis Pym was now the new Secretary of State for Northern Ireland, but it was Willie who put us all in there at first.

I took some more of that exotic concoction, when suddenly the roof of the hut began to whirl and I did not know whether it was Ash Wednesday or Pancake Tuesday. At this stage I was supposed to have done an Al Jolson impression, but everything afterwards was blank.

On Christmas morning the priest was in the Cage earlier than expected as he wanted to be back home for his Christmas dinner. I must apologise to that priest for the retorts of 'Fuck Off' by certain individuals because they thought it was a screw. All they could make out was a dark-clothed figure. My head felt as if the gong in the J. Arthur Rank films was going off in it, and my stomach was heaving.

I struggled to my locker, took out a tin of Andrews Health Salts and put some in a cup of water. My head was so sensitive to noise that I pleaded with the cup 'Please don't fizz!'

The Mass that morning was said in Irish by the priest, to responses which sounded more like Swahili.

An Interlude with Seagulls, 1982

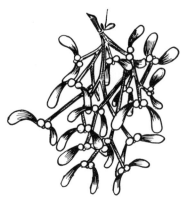

HOME ON LEAVE

Christy Brown

The little holly tree stood by the window, boy's height, in its coloured wrapping and box of clay, wired to the electric light, blazing, its tinsel glinting and bright berry-globes swaying each time somebody opened the door, making a thin metallic sound, a distant yet distinct frosty crackling sound scarcely heard above the clamour of the children in the kitchen, the hiss of logs in the fire spitting flames. In the pantry the pudding boiled and bubbled on the oven range, wrapped as always in the large flour-sack in the big corpulent copper pot, sending up clouds of steam that made the walls weep and clung to the low ceiling, to fall gradually in fat plopping drops. Paper-chains spanned the kitchen ceiling from corner to corner, shaped in hearts, flowers, rainbows, funny faces; a big ornate red and gold lotus-like star was tacked onto the old-fashioned mirror over the fireplace; in the corner above the dresser a wooden altar was erected, with a red oil-lamp on it; little china figures of the lamb and oxen, the shepherd boy and the three wise travellers were arranged round a crib that had real hay in it, the rather puzzled-looking bearded man leaning on a staff and the fragile lady with lowered eyes, all gazing at the bonny pink infant asleep in the hay. The oil-lamp played upon the ceiling and when the light was turned off it filled the kitchen with a red glow.

The two soldier-sons were home on leave, the younger one with his new girlfriend, a tall gay pretty girl named Margie, with dark hair, brown eyes, and a lovely little golden mole on her cheek, who helped Mother in the kitchen, sipped sherry, and sang snatches of songs, tossing back her long loose hair. She got down on her silk-shod knees to play with the younger kids. She laughed deep in her throat, and once she rumpled his hair with her slim nail-varnished fingers, asking him to sing with her; he smelt her clean young smell and liked her. His brother smiled blandly, every inch a cavalier, peacock-proud of her, drinking beer with a flourish out of a favourite old cracked mug, eyes on her all the time. The eldest brother drank freely now, with many a huge hiccup, and cried easily for no reason in a sentimental way, and often went in and hugged and kissed Mother as she toiled at the stove, and she would swipe at him with the towel and tell him to be grown up, and the fat foolish likeable rather lost boy who was not yet a man would wander about among the kids, crying happily and laughing, picking the little ones up and nuzzling his steamy wet face against them, playing games with them, getting down on all fours and lumbering about like an elephant, snorting with exertion, making mad outrageous animal noises till they squealed with delight, presently losing wind and puffing red-faced up again to grab his beer and gulp it down noisily.

'Here – wipe your snots and tears, you dope!' the cavalier said with a grin, tossing over a big immaculate linen hankie, showing off. He pulled his girl onto his knee and started to sing 'Margie, my little Margie'. She blushed and laughed with shy delight, tugging at his tunic collar.

From the depths of the ancient spring-loosened horsechair sofa by the burning holly tree, he watched, soaking in the magic, the fantasy that had come to life, the tremulous, uncertain joy in the room and on the familiar faces. Strange stirrings awoke in him with a fluttering and rustle of awakening wings at dawn; he sat very still, only his eyes moving, afraid to stir, as if the loud, clamorous, buzzing little room might in a moment dissolve into the old outlines of dull desolate dread. All was familiar, and all was strange; the gaudy-flowered wallpaper with new bits pasted on to hide the dirty head-stains; the ugly ceiling-high black sideboard with the many carvings and cunning little side gilt-edged mirrors, its mahogany scratched with their initials; the queer sodden brown stain on the ceiling that was somehow in the shape of a man's face like the figurings on the moon; the torn edges of the oilcloth scrubbed shiny in parts with the marks of the floorboards showing through; the hole at the bottom of the pantry door that some adven-turous midnight mouse had gnawed. . . the familiar made strange, the strange made familiar, that which was tiresomely real made dream-like, the dream descending and putting on ordinary garments, an ordinary face, dancing on ordinary feet, beckoning him, saying there was no longer need to hold back from the loud laugh and the lusty stamp of careless life-loving, telling him to come forth from that lost middle-distance, that the chains were not unbreakable, that he might enter their dusty bellowing arena, partake of their bread, share their rough warrior kit, their brawling, bruising, belligerent world, with its wordless loving and quick hating and all its screaming and sprawling mirth, its fights and heedless hurts and its mad, savage, tenacious stranglehold on life. He saw his mother's face framed in the pantry doorway, beautiful with a tired strength and innocence that escaped his groping mind. He saw the sideward-turning face of his brother's girl in the falling glow from the altar lamp, soft and dream-like on a whisper; the broad god-like knees of

93

the splendid lover, the black arrogant head hewn from burnished oak; he saw with the old lurch of heart the sad, comic, harlequin face of his eldest brother all open to the world, full of an absurd belief. He saw all this gay, hurtful life spread in generous haphazard prodigality around him like a warm sea, and he grew weak with tongueless tenderness, with the murderous longing to step over the threshold, through the waiting door, and stay forever beyond the lighted window, and never know the hunger for voyages, never heed the wind-whispered hailing call across impassable seas.

Slowly he became conscious of the hush that had settled over the room. Unwillingly dragging his time-leaping, joy-peeping thoughts back from the never-never land of possible wonder and harmony, he turned his gaze in the direction of their faces, and saw Father standing in the doorway, hatless, collar and tie loose, an expression of bemused uncertainty and confused contrition on the flushed hard-lined face, a curiously boyish look, hesitating in the doorway, as if having entered the wrong house by mistake. Nobody stirred, all talk stopped; everything seemed frozen, arrested, stilled into immobile postures, the click of a camera recording a still-life scene, as in the picturehouse sometimes when something went wrong in the projection-box and the figures would become static and wooden-like upon the screen. Mother, on her endless trips to and from the pantry, carrying a plateful of newly baked scones and apple fritters, saw him, and stopped abruptly. From away down the street some early carol singers could be heard dimly.

'You're back,' said Mother, putting down the plate on the table; her words brought movement flowing back into the room; everyone completed the gesture or motion they had been engaged in before the door opened; the eldest son put down his beer mug, the other dropped his caressing hand from his girl's hair down to her shoulder; the scrambling kids picked up their toys again.

'Don't be minding me,' said Father, coming into the kitchen, carrying a bottle under his arm; he unwrapped it ceremoniously and placed it on the table. 'For the season that's in it,' he said, then clapped his hands. 'Glasses!' he ordered, and when someone had jumped to his command and brought them from the pantry, he uncorked the bottle and poured to the brim. 'A drop of sherry, missus, for the time that's in it,' he said, handing it to her gravely. Mother, too surprised to argue or protest, took it. He turned, noticing the strange girl for the first time, his eyebrows contracting.

'Father, this is Margie,' said the dark-haired sapling son, rising with the girl, linking his arm through hers, brass buttons of uniform gleaming under the electric light. 'We're going out together.'

Father looked at them both solemnly, then grinned and poured out another glass. 'Ah, you've a bloody fine Christmas box there, sonny

94

boy!' he said, thrusting the glass into the girl's hand. 'Give her plenty of kids and she'll be happy.' He stooped and yanked one of the crawling youngsters up into his arms. 'Whoosh-a-la!' he roared, throwing the squealing, terrified child ceiling-wards and only just catching it again. 'Never let a year go by without proving who's boss!' he said, flinging the child upwards again.

'Jesus, Mary and Joseph, he'll kill me poor child!' Mother cried, rushing over and tugging the child from his arms, rocking it upon her breast, hushing its frightened cries.

'I'm as sober as a judge, missus, word of honour,' said Father, swaying back on his heels. 'Wouldn't you know just be looking at me? Ah, me poor woman!' he said with sudden desperate remorse, awkwardly rubbing her face with his thumb and forefinger, his eyes misting over. 'You've been through the mill, haven't you?' He turned to his son. 'If you've got yourself half as fine a bargain as I did thirty-odd years ago, you'll be doing bloody all right, me bucko!' he said, then turned back to Mother and put his arm around her shoulder. 'She stood by me through thick and thin and never begrudged me the price of a pint if it was in it. She has a heart of pure bloody gold, that woman, and none of yous appreciates it! Ungrateful buggers. Ah, me poor woman!' he sighed, nuzzling his face against hers and singing out in a soft unsteady voice:

Let the great big world keep turning
Never mind what may come through
For I only know that I love you so
And there's no one else but you. . .

'I'll make the tea,' said Mother, edging away, a little embarrassed in front of the girl and her grown sons. 'Sit down and rest your feet.'

'Me feet!' he said with swift nostalgia, looking down at them fondly, lifting one then the other slowly and carefully in the air; through the day-long cement-dust and muck the boot-polish still shone hard. 'I once had the best pair of dancing feet in Dublin, boys,' he said to his sons, eyes bright as pale cherries under a frosty moon. 'Ask your mother! Isn't that right, missus?' he said, grabbing her cardigan sleeve. 'Wasn't it me dancing feet that made you be me mott? D'yeh remember when we used to dance to the 'Magazine Waltz' up beyant in the oul Round Rooms of the Rotunda?' He started to whistle the tune of that far-gone unclouded time, catching hold of her hands and swirling her into the dance. 'I'm not beat yet, bejasus!' he roared exultantly, twirling her round and round in ever-widening circles, whistling madly all the time, his face shining and wild, sandy hair bushy and erect, heedless of her protests, something of summer alive in him still.

'You'll break something!' Mother gasped, trying desperately to keep her feet as he swept her faster. 'For God's sake. . .'

'He's mad,' whispered the fat eldest son, awed and scared. 'Stone mad.'

'He'd better stop it,' muttered the other tensely, clenching his fists; the girl held on to his arm tightly.

'Nineteen-eighteen. . . the Ancient Concert Rooms they were called then. . . Parnell Square. . .' Father's voice, ragged but rough with reviving memories, broke through the rhythm of his wild whistling, mounting to a shrill crescendo, his boots twinkling, beating out an erratic yet insistent drumming upon the floor, her hair tumbling and flying about her tense flushed face. 'You wore. . . a white dress. . . red ribbons in your hair. . . little black shoes. . . O Jesus, we were young. . .'

The Christmas tree toppled over on its side as they inexorably crashed into it, falling with a bang and hiss of crackling exploding fairylights, its gay little glass globes rolling over the floor, the box of clay splitting and spilling out; the bottle of sherry went over as somebody bumped against the table; the room plummeted into sudden darkness save for the weird red radiance from the little oil-lamp on the altar; the children whimpered and began to cry as their toys were stepped on in the sudden chaos of frantic feet and muttered curses, which was followed by a strange and baffled silence.

'Jesus,' said Father softly, hoarsely, sprawled amid the ruins of the festive tree, passing a trembling hand over his forehead.

The carol singers were closer now, almost outside the front gate, clear voices rising in the cold brilliant night air, singing '*Adeste Fideles*'.

Down All the Days, 1970

DR CROKE'S CHRISTMAS PARTY

William O'Brien

Our Christmas dinner party was as simple and joyous as the circle around His Grace's table was always sure to be. 'The victuals,' as he loved to call them, were of the best, and so were the wines within a modest compass; but all else was of minor account in the glow of his own bulk and big assemblance at the head of the table – genial, appreciative, overflowing with high spirits and unwounding raillery – a schoolboy and a great man gloriously combined to give his guests the sensation of a summer sun warming us in a little firmament of our own, while the frost and snow were making the world howl and shudder outside.

One of the Christmas party was a little Augustinian priest – whom the Archbishop called affectionately 'George' or 'the Friar' or 'the Hermit' – who, I suspect, was indebted to His Grace's privy purse for the means of sustaining the small convent of Austin Hermits of which he was now the only surviving Hermit. I am quite sure it was out of tenderness for his solitary condition he was bidden to the warmth of the Archiepiscopal Christmas board. His Grace bantered the Friar with the unfailing good humour which saves the rough-and-tumble pleasantries among Irish priests in their convivial moments from ever degenerating into malice or anger. The Friar listened with a twinkle in his rolling eye, cleared up his trencher of roast turkey or plum pudding with a gentle joy, and, imitating the revenge of Souwarow on a famous occasion 'made no answer,' but, after dinner, relieved the cleverest of his tormentors of their sixpences at the game of 'nap'. Not, however, the Archbishop, who walked round the table inspecting the players' hands and now and again helped a lame dog over the stile by an expert hint, but, so far as my experience went, never took a hand himself.

Between Charlie Tanner and His Grace – both of them models of physical strength which under the chisel of an Athenian sculptor might have lived as miracles in marble – their common passion for athletics would have been an all-sufficient bond. They talked boxing, and Tanner, true to his French training, defended the head thrust in the stomach as legitimate as well as effective warfare, while Dr Croke mentioned that he had himself once punished that mode of attack on the part of a Frenchman by a sound kicking of another inferior and still less noble part of the body below the belt.

They were both fanatics for handball. Dr Croke regretted he did not know it while daylight lasted as he should have challenged Charlie to a match against the garden wall of the Archiepiscopal Palace. But hurling was the Archbishop's grand passion in the matter of Irish sports. It had

all the intoxication of battle and had kept Irish soldiership alive during the Penal ages, when the people were stripped of their last battleaxe or gun. Even the faction fighting of old he spoke of not without softness as a sort of battle exercised when there was no better to be had, and *a propos* mentioned that in the onsets between Tipperary and Cork long ago, the brawny giants of Tipperary who generally had the upper hand used to say of a man whose skull was cracked with undue facility: 'That fellow has a Cork skull,' to which the Cork retort used to be: 'Yes, a Cork skull has some brains to be knocked out.'

The Catholic Bulletin, April 1920

LETTER TO LADY GREGORY

Sean O'Casey

Kensington
Christmas Eve 1926

My dear Lady Gregory,

I suppose you think (forgive me for not writing to you) I have allowed former memories to be submerged by Glamour of London. I haven't, & feelings for & remembrance of you are as deeply affectionate as ever.

I am living here as quietly as I have lived in Dublin; abiding alone even throughout the Christmas Festival. I am now – very tranquilly – working on a new play.

Keeping away from dinners, luncheons, parties & dances prevents me from doing very much for the Lane Pictures. Augustus John & I have come to be very fond of each other.

I have just got from him a lovely 'Head of a Girl', which I shall keep during my life, & then – if they will take it from me – I will give it to the Dublin M. Art Gallery, or, if you like, to be added to the Lane Collection.

Up to the present this is all I can do for Dublin.

I sincerely hope the Abbey is doing well.

'The Whiteheaded Boy' is doing splendidly here.

Please give my love to all my worker friends in Coole.

Affectionately Yours,

Sean.

The Letters of Sean O'Casey, volume 1, 1910–41, 1975

CHRISTMAS AT THE FRONT, 1914

John Harold M'Ervel

Xmas Eve

I am for outpost tonight (i.e. C. Coy. is), and tomorrow we dig out, sometime in the afternoon, for heaven knows where. It doesn't look like a Christmas dinner tomorrow night, but still things are going all right, and I'm having a jolly good time. This morning I was out in front seeing the exact line to be taken up tonight, and I discovered a deserted cottage that will do as company HQ, and as there is a piano it should be very cheery. Of course it wouldn't do to occupy such a prominent place permanently, else you would be spotted, and the place blown up with shell-fire, but it will be quite safe for one night. There were chickens at the farm, and my orderly and I caught a couple, and cut their heads off with an old French bayonet. Coming home in great triumph, I with a bloody bayonet, and the man with two hens, who should we meet but the Colonel and Major Stevenson. There were some comments on the proclivities of the Irish for looting, but it was only jealousy. We had a great evening last night, as we had B Company for dinner and a concert afterwards. Finally to bed on the straw with an old blanket over me and deep sleep for eight or nine hours. It's like old times to hear again the zip of the bullets, and the crash of the guns. Thank goodness the Germans don't seem to have much artillery at this point – very different to Ypres. The Indians are here, and I'm never tired of watching them and trying to talk to them. They have soft, pleasant voices, but it's only a few who can speak very broken English. Their transport is a very ramshackle collection of mule carts, but I understand very efficient.

Xmas Day

I'm going up to the trenches any moment now. We are just waiting for the appearance of certain troops we are relieving, as it doesn't do to block up a communicating trench by having troops trying to get along in different directions at the same time. Today was a glorious hard, frosty Christmas, and everyone seemed in good humour for no apparent reason. I had a great Christmas Eve. Went on outpost at dusk – about 4 p.m. – and stayed on till 8, when the next relief came up. Usual business, leaning up against the side of a trench and talking to your neighbour and listening to the sniping and an occasional gun; there was no heavy firing. It was a clear moonlight night, and no danger of a rush. At eight I returned to the outposts' HQ, about 100 yards down the road, and had a great evening. A table with a white cloth waited me there, and some very splendid soup, followed by my fowl and coffee, and such put us in great heart, and we started the piano, and in half an hour the little room was full of Gascons and a couple of Highlanders, all singing away. I left at midnight for another spell on the post, and most of the next four hours I spent sleeping in a barrel. The Gascons were great fellows, rather like operatic tenors in appearance – all fierce moustaches and beards, but they sang party songs splendidly. Myself, I sang a bit also.

The Letters of John Harold M'Ervel (Major), 1916

HOLLY

Michael Walsh

The year is young when she comes in daisies
Frail wings of white in the April dew,
Her heart is high in its princely promise
Tinting the valley with bells of blue.

But all her glory of blossom ended,
Her Joy of Morning is yet to be
When out of the mists and moors of winter
She comes in red to the holly tree.

Red on the Holly

A MIDNIGHT MASS

Michael J. Murphy

It was very quiet out here on the road in the hills; a quiet uninfluenced by the mystery of the night with stars tracing the infinite canopy of the sky and ancient Slieve Gullion in the north, black, reticent, mysterious, converging with space, giving benediction to that quiet. Before me, on an arm of the mountain itself, rose the night-darkened church of St Patrick's, Dromintee, South Armagh. The quiet was like an intangible, infinite thing at rest but not sleeping. It was Christmas Eve. In a little over half an hour Midnight Mass would be celebrated in that Chapel now wrapped in the darkness of the night.

I was practically alone. Pipe bowls winked at the stars now and then. I could hear human voices, but could not see anybody. Hills and mountains, crouching fantastically in the darkness, walled in the valley and its inspiring quietude. All over the valley and on the hills candles burned in every window of the dwellings in cheery profusion. This lighting of candles in every window is a very ancient custom of Christmas still observed by these people.

Hands which had often placed lighted candles in those windows had helped to build this solemn edifice looming in the darkness over the graveyard, where many of them now rested. It was a thought bearing an ineffable peacefulness and not a sad thought.

Slieve Gullion watched with hidden eyes that made themselves felt, the personality of the mountain. If that mountain could speak! It would tell of hidden Mass Rocks up amid the boulders and heather where, perhaps, Mass had been celebrated even on Christmas Eve. It could tell of Blessed Oliver Plunket hiding in the cairn on the summit from his enemies. . .

The deep boom of the Chapel bell, the first bell, smashes in on thought and reverie, and for a moment the trance-like quietude of the valley has been disturbed. I am no longer practically alone; intangible groups stand on the road and sit on the ditch of grey stone, their voices purring softly.

A light appears amid the heather on Slieve Gullion; it is a 'lamp-thorn', or hurricane-lamp, borne by one of a party coming in single-file along an ancient path or 'pad' as they call it. Heather brushing their boots springs from ground redolent with history. The sound of a horse's hoofs rhythm metallically over the still air. The bell moans itself into reluctant silence. More lights appear on the hills to the south, where the section of the range is outlined against the glare in the sky from the town lights of Dundalk. More and still more footsteps crunch on loose stones, but figures are still intangible silhouettes.

In a flash the darkness around me has been dispelled as a light over the Gothic doorway springs into brilliancy with a blatant glare, which momentarily dazzles and contracts one's eyes. Two old figures alighting from an ass-drawn cart stare at the new wonder with mild alarm. . . the old man nods his white head resignedly at a marvel of a strange and, to him, bewildering era. He remembers the rush-candles. Together they pass through the portals. It was a touching scene.

Ghostly fingers enshrouded in a gauzy substance stab the darkness of the heavens; they are the headlights of cars speeding up hills from all directions towards the Chapel – sometimes the headlights form an arch of light. The cars, out of tune with the quiet, slide to halt beside a lethargic ass tethered to a stunted tree, and their headlights reveal the candle-lamp on the ass-cart. Exhaust smoke swirls through the glare almost like rain rushing through a shaft of light from a window. Women in black shawls flit by, the shawls cowl-like drawn over their faces. Some of the men are clad in overcoats, others in solid navy-blue and cloth-caps. There is a continual undertone of conversation, an audible murmuring. The last bell drowns every other human sound. It is within a few minutes of midnight on Christmas Eve.

Away up on the surrounding hills I know that there are other people patiently awaiting the boom of that last bell to transport them in spirit to the Chapel on the hill below. When the last boom of the bell had moaned itself into silence they would fix their eyes on that electric light gleaming in the darkness below like a big star – symbolic of another star – cross themselves, bow their aged heads and pray.

Around that light all is quiet again – the quiet of an inspiring spectacle; not that spectacle which belongs to fanfaronade or pageantry, but the greater spectacle inherent in a solemn devotion. I go in to Midnight Mass in this Chapel in the hills of the north.

At Slieve Gullion's Foot, 1975

SANTA CLAUS NEEDS A HELPING HAND

Donal Foley

Irish children this year may be without their traditional Christmas morning visitor. Santa Claus has demanded a helper to carry his sack while he drives his sleigh. Otherwise he will strike, and he is supported by members of the National Sleigh Drivers Union. Santa would also like a rearranged time schedule. 'A day shift, rather than all this furtive night work,' he said.

Said Senator Michael Mullen of the ITGWU: 'We have instructed our own members to support the sleigh drivers. I cannot, however, speak for the NBU.'

Children all over Ireland expressed support for Santa Claus last night. They had rooftop meetings in many parts of the country, and some were carrying stones in their stockings as well. The Taoiseach, Mr Cosgrave, gave a pledge that Christmas would not be abandoned, but would go on as normal. He added that if Santa Claus persisted in his strike, members of the Cabinet would stand in for him and come down the chimneys themselves. 'We will not have the country held to ransom by a doddering old fool,' he said.

Mr Liam St John Bosco Devlin, Chairman of CIE, said that if the worst happened, his own organisation would supply a skeleton Santa Claus service in the same way as they had been supplying a skeleton bus service for years.

Man Bites Dog, 1977

104

AN ECLOGUE FOR CHRISTMAS

Louis MacNeice

A. I meet you in an evil time.
B.   The evil bells
   Put out of our heads, I think, the thought of every
       thing else.
A. The jaded calendar revolves,
   Its nuts need oil, carbon chokes the valves,
   The excess sugar of a diabetic culture
   Rotting the nerve of life and literature;
   Therefore when we bring out the old tinsel and frills
   To announce that Christ is born among the
       barbarous hills
   I turn to you whom a morose routine
   Saves from the mad vertigo of being what has been.
B. Analogue of me, you are wrong to turn to me,
   My country will not yield you any sanctuary,
   There is no pinpoint in any of the ordnance maps
   To save you when your towns and town-bred
       thoughts collapse,
   It is better to die *in situ* as I shall,
   One place is as bad as another. Go back where your
       instincts call
   And listen to the crying of the town-cats and the
       taxis again,
   Or wind your gramophone and eavesdrop on great men.
A. Jazz-weary of years of drums and Hawaiian guitar,

Pivoting on the parquet I seem to have moved far
From bombs and mud and gas, have stuttered on
        my feet
Clinched to the streamlined and butter-smooth
        trulls of the élite,
The lights irritating and gyrating and rotating in
        gauze –
Pomade–dazzle, a slick beauty of gewgaws –
I who was Harlequin in the childhood of the
        century,
Posed by Picasso beside an endless opaque sea,
Have seen myself sifted and splintered in broken
        facets,
Tentative pencillings, endless liabilities, no assets,
Abstractions scalpelled with a palette-knife
Without reference to this particular life.
And so it has gone on; I have not been allowed
        to be
Myself in flesh or face, but abstracting and
        dissecting me
They have made of me pure form, a symbol or a
        pastiche,
Stylised profile, anything but soul and flesh:
And that is why I turn this jaded music on
To forswear thought and become an automaton.
B. There are in the country also of whom I am afraid –
Men who put beer into a belly that is dead,
Women in the forties with terrier and setter who
        whistle and swank
Over down and plough and Roman road and
        daisied bank,
Half-conscious that these barriers over which they
        stride
Are nothing to the barbed wire that has grown
        round their pride.
A. And two there are, as I drive in the city, who
        suddenly perturb –
The one sirening me to draw up by the kerb
The other, as I lean back, my right leg stretched
        creating speed,
Making me catch and stamp, the brakes shrieking,
        pull up dead:
She wears silk stockings taunting the winter
        wind,

He carries a white stick to mark that he is blind
B. In the country they are still hunting, in the heavy
    shires
   Greyness is on the fields and sunset like a line of
    pyres
   Of barbarous heroes smoulders through the ancient
    air
   Hazed with factory dust and, orange opposite, the
    moon's glare,
   Goggling yokel-stubborn through the iron trees,
   Jeers at the end of us, our bland ancestral ease;
   We shall go down like palaeolithic man
   Before some new Ice Age or Genghiz Khan.
A. It is time for some new coinage, people have got so old,
   Hacked and handled and shiny from pocketing
    they have made bold
   To think that each is himself through these
    accidents, being blind
   To the fact that they are merely the counters of
    an unknown Mind.
B. A Mind that does not think, if such a thing can be,
   Mechanical Reason, capricous Identity.
   That I could be able to face this domination nor
    flinch –
A. The tin toys of the hawker move on the pavement
    inch by inch
   Not knowing that they are wound up; it is better
    to be so
   Than to be, like us, wound up and while running
    down to know –
B. But everywhere the pretence of individuality
    recurs –
A. Old faces frosted with powder and choked in furs.
B. The jutlipped farmer gazing over the humpbacked
    wall.
A. The commercial traveller joking in the urinal.
B. I think things draw to an end, the soil is stale.
A. And over-elaboration will nothing now avail,
   The street is up again, gas, electricity or drains,
   Ever-changing conveniences, nothing comfortable
    remains,
   Unimproved, as flagging Rome improved villa and
    sewer
   (A sound-proof library and a stable temperature).

Our street is up, red lights sullenly mark
The long trench of pipes, iron guts in the dark,
And not till the Goths again come swarming down
    the hill
Will cease the clangour of the pneumatic drill.
But yet there is beauty narcotic and deciduous
In this vast organism grown out of us:
On all the traffic-islands stand white globes like
    moons,
The city's haze is clouded amber that purrs and
    croons,
And tilting by the noble curve bus after tall bus
    comes
With an osculation of yellow light, with a glory
    like chrysanthemums.

B.   The country gentry cannot change, they will die in
    their shoes
From angry circumstance and moral self-abuse,
Dying with a paltry fizzle they will prove their
    lives to be
An ever-diluted drug, a spiritual tautology.
They cannot live once their idols are turned out,
None of them can endure, for how could they,
    possibly, without
The flotsam of private property, Pekingese and
    polyanthus,
The good things which in the end turn to poison
    and pus,
Without the bandy chairs and the sugar in the silver
    tongs
And the inter-ripple and resonance of years of
    dinner-gongs?
Or if they could find no more that cumulative
    proof
In the rain dripping off the conservatory roof?
What will happen when the only sanction the
    country-dweller has –

A.   What will happen to us, planked and panelled with
    jazz?
Who go to the theatre where a black man dances
    like an eel,
Where pink thighs flash like the spokes of a wheel,
    where we feel
That we know in advance all the jogtrot and the

cakewalk jokes
All the bumfun and the gags of the comedians in
     boaters and toques,
All the tricks of the virtuosos who invert the usual –

B. What will happen to us when the State takes down
     the manor wall,
When there is no more private shooting or fishing,
     when the trees are all cut down,
When faces are all dials and cannot smile or frown –

A. What will happen when the sniggering machine-
     guns in the hands of the young men
Are trained on every flat and club and beauty
     parlour and Father's den?
What will happen when our civilisation like a long
     pent balloon –

B. What will happen will happen; the whore and the
     buffoon
Will come off best; no dreamers, they cannot lose
     their dream
And are at least likely to be reinstated in the new
    regime,
But one thing is not likely –

A.   Do not gloat over yourself
Do not be your own vulture, high on some mountain
     shelf
Huddle the pitiless abstractions bald about the neck
Who will descend when you crumple in the plains a
     wreck.
Over the randy of the theatre and cinema I hear
     songs
Unlike anything –

B.   The lady of the house poises the silver tongs
And picks a lump of sugar, *'ne plus ultra'* she says,
'I cannot do otherwise, even to prolong my days' –

A. I cannot do otherwise either, tonight I will book my
     seat –

B. I will walk about the farm-yard which is replete
As with the smell of dung so with memories –

A. I will gorge myself to satiety with the oddities
Of every artiste, official or amateur,
Who has pleased me in my rôle of hero-worshipper
Who has pleased me in my rôle of individual man –

B. Let us lie once more, say 'What we think, we can' –
The old idealist lie –

A.   And for me before I die
Let me go the round of the garish glare –
B.   And on the bare and high
Places of England, the Wiltshire Downs and the
       Long Mynd
Let the balls of my feet bounce on the turf, my face
       burn in the wind
My eyelashes stinging in the wind, and the sheep like
       grey stones
Humble my human pretensions –
A.   Let the saxophones and the xylophones
And the cult of every technical excellence, the
       miles of canvas in the galleries
And the canvas of the rich man's yacht snapping and
       tacking on the seas
And the perfection of a grilled steak –
B.   Let all these so ephemeral things
Be somehow permanent like the swallow's tangent
       wings:
Goodbye to you, this day remember is Christmas,
       this morn
They say, interpret it your own way, Christ is born.

Selected Poems, 1963

PATROLLING AT CHRISTMASTIME

John McGahern

He was with Mullins. At eleven they had started to clear the pubs, meeting hostility and resentment in every house, and in McDermott's at the church a familiar arm was put round Mullins's neck and he was told, 'Never mind the auld duty, John. Have a drink on the house, forget it all, it'll taste just as sweet in the uniform.' The invitation was greeted by a storm of cheering. Mullins was furious and Reegan had to order him to be still. When the cheering died Reegan said, 'I'm givin' every man three minutes to get off these premises. I'll summons every man on these premises in three minutes' time.'

He spoke with quiet firmness: a sullen muttering rose but they gulped their drinks and left.

'No respect for anything, just like the bloody animals in the fields,' Mullins was muttering as the pub cleared, and he gave full vent to his rage on a man they found pissing in public against the churchyard wall as they came out.

'Get out of it,' Mullins roared in a fury of assertion.

'Sugar off home outa that with yourself and mind your own business,' the man swayed erect to mutter, certain it was someone trying to joke him out of his position or else a puritan madman he was determined to put in his place. In a flash Mullins was beside him with drawn baton. 'Get out of it. Have you no shame, young girls passin' here to Mass, or are you an animal?'

'You wouldn't mind handlin' those fillies closer than ever my pissin'll get to them, you narrow-minded auld bastard,' the drunk shouted as he buttoned his fly, and a cheer went up from the outhouses.

'What did you say to *me*? What did you say? Do you see *this*?' Mullins thrust the baton before the man's face, gripping him by the shoulder, mad with rage. 'Do you know what this is? Would you like a taste of this?'

'No,' the man jabbered, the hard wood of the baton against his face, and he saw the silver buttons, the peaked cap: he was dealing with the police. Painfully the drunken brains was made to function in the space of seconds: he'd be up in court; his name would be in the newspapers; he'd be the laughing-stock of the country.

'I'm sorry,' he tried to slide. 'I'm sorry. I didn't know. I'm sorry.'

'You're sorry now! It's never too late to be sorry, is it? You weren't that a minute ago and young girls pass this way to Mass, you know! And what kind of language was that you were usin' to officers of the law? Do you see this? Do you see this, do you? Would you like to get the tannin' you deserve with this and find yourself in court later?' Mullins ground threateningly with the baton, but growing placated, he was master now.

The man watched the baton close to his face, the shock had left him cold sober beneath the depression of alcohol, he was past caring what happened now, he shivered, he hoped it was all a passing nightmare. The cheering had died in the outhouses. Reegan moved close for the first time.

'What's your name?' Reegan demanded.

The name was hopelessly given.

'What do you do?'

'A sawyer.'

Reegan knew the man's name, what his work was, but the demanding of the information was an old bullying trick policemen learn and it had become a habit by this time.

'Shouldn't you know better than to be at something like that,' he began in the official moral tone, but grew disgusted, and with an impatient movement told him to be gone. Mullins had subsided into approving growls, but, as the man made good his escape, woke to shout, 'Get home outa that you disgraceful blaguard and never let me catch you at that in public again.' Reegan watched Mullins coldly: the cheeks seemed flushed in the weak light of the candles in the windows.

'Such a disgrace and young girls passin'. Such language. No better than the animals in the fields.' Mullins tried to justify himself to Reegan, who only smiled sardonically at the moral indignation, remembering Mullins's gloating stories of the gunshot nights and through blood and sand and shit MacGregory will ride tonight.

A mad surge of strength rose in Reegan, desire to break the whole mess up into its first chaos; there was no order, only the police force. He sent Mullins to the church gate to help Casey direct the traffic, he said he'd do the last round of the village on his own. He felt the naked baton in his own pocket and began to curse as he walked away.

It was later than two in the Christmas morning when they were finished: the last of the cars directed away from the church, the roads patrolled for drunks, the reports filled into the books in the dayroom.

No one slept on the iron bed against the wall of the lockup during Christmas. Reegan put a chair against the door so that he'd be able to hear the phone or anyone knocking from his own bedroom. He drank the barley water that Elizabeth had left covered beside the raked fire, believing that it cleansed his blood, something he'd brought with him from his childhood. Then he climbed the stairs in his stockinged feet, carrying the green glass oil-lamp, and placed a boot quietly against the bedroom door to make sure it stayed open. Elizabeth was awake. 'Is it late?' she asked.

The Barracks, 1963

THE HAUNTED RECTORY

St John D. Seymour and Harry Nelligan

A well-known Canon (since retired) in the Diocese of Clogher writes as
follows:

'On Christmas Eve 1885 my attention was directed by my cook to a
curious noise, somewhat like what a very heavily-laden wagon passing
close to a rather rickety house would make. At first I gave but little heed
to her alarm; to be quite candid, I suspected the presence of a tipsy
sweetheart, and it being the Festive Season I did *not* want to know
everything. However, the woman's manner betokened sincerity and
genuine fear of something, so I called my man-servant, and we descended, a dauntless three, to the kitchen. Arrived there we found the
vibrating noise to increase strongly, and the whole basement of the
house to be in a condition suggestive of the working of an earthquake,
but without any of the furniture or dishes being moved or in any way
disturbed. Two brilliant lamps, one on the wall and the other on the
table in the middle of the rather small kitchen, afforded light almost as
clear as daylight. We three stood in amazement at what was, without
any visible cause, going on around us, the servants literally clinging to
me, one on either side.

'The noise suddenly ceased, both as regards our immediate vicinity
and its hitherto rumbling character, while a pantry right in front of
which we stood became the scene of fresh disturbances. There it seemed
as if china, dishes, and glass were being thrown with tremendous
violence on the flagged floor. As soon as each crash resounded in our
ears the terrified domestics clung with intense fervour to my arms.
Convinced now of the fact that some "game" was being played on me,
of which my servants were the sharers, if not the actual devisers, I
resolved to open the pantry door, which was locked but had the key in
it, and investigate the mystery, if such it should prove to be. But my
suggestion simply threw my panic-stricken companions almost into fits,
and they implored me not to do so. I replied to them: "Yes, in God's
name I *will* open the door, and if you two are too cowardly to follow me, I
shall go in by myself, and discover the secret of all the confusion."
Accordingly I made a quick and very energetic movement towards the
scene of the mysterious noise, *when slowly the locked door of the pantry
opened,* and out glided a tall female figure, dressed in a loose white dress,
with a short black cape round her shoulders. I was literally paralysed
with fright. My now almost frantic servants gripped me by each arm as
in a vice, causing me intense pain, and, as it subsequently turned out,

114

leaving the marks of their grips for many days in the fleshy part of my arms. It was to this sharp physical pain I attribute the passing away of the feeling of faintness caused by the apparition, and the restoration to a state of comparative coolness.

'I rushed after the figure, which continued to move towards the stairs, which as soon as she had reached she vanished from sight. Scarcely had she done so when my two little boys at the top of the house, three stories higher than where I stood, screamed out, "There is a woman in white in the room with us." I literally fled up to the boys' room, followed by my two sharers of the vision. On arriving there I closely questioned the children. The eldest, aged ten, told me he had lain awake to watch for Santa Claus, but instead of the genial old Children's Friend he saw a strange lady, who just glided into the room and out again, leaving no toys, nor any other trace of her presence. Every place was searched without avail, but no token of our strange visitor was found. The pantry door was *still locked*, and on its being opened no sign of anything having been disturbed was discoverable.

'Since then the same visitant has been seen by myself, by other members of the family, and by visitors.'

True Irish Ghost Stories, 1966

AFTER PHILIPHAUGH

Rev. George Hill

In the interval between the battle of Philiphaugh and December, many of the Scottish nobility and gentry who had fought in the ranks of the royalist army were taken prisoners. On 5 December, a commission from the General Assembly of the church presented a 'Remonstrance' to the Estates or Scottish Parliament, complaining that the delays in the execution of the prisoners of war were displeasing to the Supreme Judge of all the earth, dangerous unto themselves (the members of Parliament), and grievous unto the hearts of the Lord's people! . . .

Such ghastly counsels produced the bloodiest results – results so shocking that at last the scaffold came to be called the 'Covenant Shambles'. Such of the hapless Irish as were not slaughtered at Philiphaugh, were done to death in due course subsequently. Two of their most distinguished officers, Colonel Manus O'Cahan and Major Lachlan, had greatly endeared themselves to Montrose by their gallantry and fidelity. They commanded at Philiphaugh, where, instead of being massacred with their soldiers, they were studiously reserved for a more lingering and ignominious fate. The Covenanters wished to have an exhibition of triumph in the capital, so these officers were sent forward to Edinburgh, and hanged on the Castle Hill, without even the semblance of a trial. Several Irish, including women and children, made their escape before the general massacre at Philiphaugh, and were soon afterwards captured along the line of Leslie's march. This brutal fellow was accompanied by a committee of estates appointed to assist him in deciding all doubtful points that might arise; he also benefitted by the presence of several preachers, who never failed, when Irish captives were brought in, to urge their immediate execution. At one point in the line of march, these preachers must have felt that their exhortations were not given in vain. Wishart records that Irish stragglers 'being gathered together, were thrown headlong from off a high bridge; and the men, together with their wives and children, drowned in the river beneath; and if any chanced to swim towards the side, they were beaten off with pikes and staves, and thrust down again into the water'. The Covenanting soldiers, guilty of these barbarities, were braced up to their bloody work by the preachers, who kept repeating the following, among other passages of Scripture, supposed to countenance their atrocious conduct: 'What meaneth, then, this bleating of sheep in my ears, and the lowing of the oxen? Thine eye shall not pity, and thou shalt not spare.' But the Covenant soldiers did not require to be stirred up in the matter, for they had, as they felt, many defeats now to avenge on these hated

Irish; indeed during Montrose's campaigns the soldiers of the Covenant, by defeats as invariable as they were ignominious, had become absolutely frantic. In addition to the Irish caught on the line of Leslie's march, there were many who had escaped in other directions, but who were also eventually captured on 26 December, 1646; immediately after the petitions received from the Synods of Merse and Teviotdale, Fife, Dumfries, and Galloway – 'The House ordains the Irish prisoners taken at and after Philiphaugh, in all the prisons of the kingdom, especially in the prisons of Selkirk, Jedburgh, Glasgow, Dumbarton, and Perth, *to be executed without any assize or process,* conform to the treaty betwixt both kingdoms passed in act.' 'These,' says Napier, 'were only the gleanings of that glorious harvest day of the Covenant. There was no treaty between the kingdoms (England and Scotland) that touched the case. That was a miserable subterfuge, a flimsy phraseology, by which conscious cruelty sought to cloak a cowardly crime.'

The MacDonnells of Antrim, 1873

CHRISTMAS

Padraig Ó Siochfhradha

I must tell you about the Christmas we had. Mam went to Dingle a few days before it – herself and Dad – and they took the horse and cart, with a creel and a box in the cart.

Mam had the money, and she took two geese – one for the vet and one for the bank manager, because he's the man who minds her money and she thinks the world of him.

While they were in Dingle, I went off to Glenadown with the big knife and some string and brought home a big holly bush, and I got some ivy in the ruins of the church.

As I was passing her door, Nell Mary Andy came out and was buttering me up trying to get me to give her some holly. She thought she'd make a right little eejit of me praising me and calling me a 'good little boy', and promising me a Christmas present! I pretended, at first, that I wouldn't give her any. But, when I untied the bundle at home, I took a couple of branches over. I'm very great with Nell, you know.

Cait was all excited when she saw the big load I was bringing in.

– Oh! said she, we'll make the house lovely, and she was looking at the red berries on the holly and dancing around the floor.

– Oh, aren't they beautiful? said she. Did you ever see such a lovely red?

That's the way Cait always goes on, even if it's only a daisy or a bunch of cowslips. All the girls are like that, about all kinds of things.

I was hungry.

– Stop your messing, said I, is there anything to eat?

– Oh! I forgot, said Cait and she began to whisper. You won't tell what I've made, will you?

– What? said I.

She laughed.

– I won't tell you, because you'd tell Mam.

– I swear I won't, said I.

She'll kill me over the sugar, said Cait.

– What sugar? said I.

– And because of the cream! said she.

– Crikey, Cait, have you made sweet cakes!

118

– I won't tell you, I won't tell you, said she, laughing and jumping up and down. Then she went to the dresser and took down two cups.

– Ah! Cait, said I, tell me what you made.

– I won't, I won't, said she, and she laughed, dancing and kicking up her heels. She didn't see the ivy on the floor until it tripped her up and, lo and behold, didn't she break a big piece off the rim of one of the cups.

Cait picked it up and she was trembling as she tried to fix it back in place. She started to cry, and then didn't she try to put the blame on me! I soon told her that it was herself and her jumping around. But there was no point in talking. All she'd do was cry.

I ended up feeling sorry for her.

– Give it to me, Cait, said I, and Mam won't ever know about it.

I took the cup to the dresser and put it under two other cups with the broken side facing in.

– What will I do if Mam finds it? said Cait.

Then we each had a mug of tea. That was when Cait brought out the things she'd made – little cream cakes with sugar icing on them. We got butter in the cupboard and I spotted a big pot of jam with the top tied tight. I cut the knot easily and we enjoyed all the things we had. We put a full spoon of jam on every bit of bread.

When we'd eaten our fill, the jam was well down the pot, but I tied the paper on again and put it back in the cupboard where it had been. It's a pity Mam doesn't go to Dingle every day!

Then I got a hammer and little nails and Cait handed me the holly and ivy. We nailed it around the window, on top of the dresser, and over the fireplace. It was hard to fix it where there was no wood, and I had to drive big nails into the wall. From time to time huge chunks of mortar fell.

When we'd finished the house, we grabbed Sailor – that's the dog – and covered him from head to tail with holly, and had a great laugh at him. When evening came we lit the lamp. The house looked lovely.

It was dark when Mam and Dad came home. We thought Mam'd be delighted but, to tell the truth, she caused ructions when she saw the lumps of mortar missing from the walls. I had to disappear until she calmed down. It's hard to please some people!

Jimeen, 1984

ROAMING THE FIELDS ON BOXING DAY

Sam Hanna Bell

'Let the hare sit,' said the huntsman. It is a phrase of the chase rubbed so smooth that I had always thought it was a proverb. But I heard it used in its pristine sense one needle-sharp Boxing Day in a field outside Tassagh. I had been trailing behind three men as they crept up the ditch that bounded the field. We were looking for a hare and I didn't want to be the one to find it. So I followed at a distance not letting my gaze wander too far on either side. Suddenly the huntsman stopped: 'Let the hare sit,' he said over his shoulder. He must have thought I was on his heels for his companions didn't need the advice. He crouched and crept backwards a few steps and then turned. 'I have her lying!' he crowed and at that moment I saw the hare leave her den and go away across the field in a precise and beautiful arc. The man let a great guldher out of him and we heard the hounds and horns explode from the hollow below the field in which we stood.

To enjoy a hunt one must presumably either run with the hare or hunt with the hounds. But there is also a less energetic and indeed if you wish neutral position in which you can dispose yourself to follow the sport. That is to climb to a hilltop and watch the hunt

For as the hare whom hounds and horns pursue
Pants to the place from whence at first she flew

it is possible by moving from hill to hill to keep the hare and hounds in view as they sweep the countryside in a circle – a circle drawn by the hunted animal.

It's no affectation on my part to suggest that the hare enjoys the hunt. I've been told so by a score of men who have followed their dogs for two score years through the fields of Armagh, Tyrone, Fermanagh and Monaghan. They do not seek the hare's life. Indeed, if he is obviously flagging the dogs are 'run-off'. But this is not so easy, for a tired hare gives off a heavier scent and the pursuit and cry of the hounds when they know that their quarry is losing pace becomes 'wickeder'. It's only in the past few years when hares have become more plentiful that the huntsmen have tolerated in the chase that cretin of the canine world, the greyhound. A shotgun is still the weapon of the barbarian.

Now all this was to me a nuance, for I come from a part of the Province where sportsmen justify hunting in so far as it can be justified by eating what they kill, vermin excepted. (Apart, that is, from some preposterous individuals on horseback who used to arrive in the district with a stag enclosed in a thing like a pantechnicon. This unhappy beast was released and chased across the townland until the 'hunters' had had enough. It was then secured again by underlings and hoisted back into the conveyance and driven away. I have no doubt that the stag enjoyed being hunted. Man's ego makes him remarkably adroit in interpreting animal behaviour.)

'The whole purpose of the hunt is *not* to kill the hare but to see the hounds working,' the Armagh man will tell you, not without impatience if you persist in thinking that a hare's chief end is *Timbale de Lièvre.*

The stranger, of course, will be unable to appreciate the finer points of the hound-work. Nor will he until he has talked to an experienced hunter be able to appreciate the wiles and stratagems of the hare.

The hounds are usually bred and maintained by farmers who bring them along on the day of the hunt to make the pack. It is this individual ownership which introduced rivalry between the hounds apart from the contest of life and death between the hounds and the hare. Not only can the experienced huntsman, out of view but within earshot, tell how the chase is flowing through the hills, but listening to the cry of the pack he can tell which hound is hot on the hare's heels. And so noted hounds have their names embedded in balladry:

> As they flew over yonder hill
>   It was a lovely sight.
> There was dogs black and yellow
> There was dogs black and white
> The bouncing hare she did her best
>   Upon that frosty ground
> When that great dog from Killileagh
>   Brave Rattler took her down.

Danger deviseth shifts; wit waits on fear. And sympathy no less pre-supposes knowledge. I came away from the winter fields of Tassagh impressed by the enthusiasm and gaiety of the hunters, but for me much of the attraction of the hunt remains a cold scent. It appeared nothing more or less than a small and graceful animal (in Irish the hare is 'garrey' or little deer) pursued by a crowd of men with the best intentions – and a pack of hounds.

Erin's Orange Lily, 1956

WORK ON WREN'S DAY

John Ennis

Saint Stephen's Day
You found us work to do
Digging lightly around the apple trees.
Beneath a fresh snow-blue pallor
The wind whipped its new steel comb
Through the touselled silver branches.
A few yellow-red apples
Clung on to boughs that were rambling
And dormant with cloven buds.
The hoarse sound of our spades
Loosened up the cold soaked clay.
Boredom and resentment
Smouldered blackly in me.
Spring, like Christmas,
Stretched light years away.
A wren studied us from a branch,
Ate at a distance worms we unearthed.
At our clay-caked boots as we dug
We kept the sharp eye for snowdrops
Wild hyacinths, and the premature green
Blades of the daffodil.

A touch of frost fingered like a thief
Cut into the cold clamour of sweat on our necks,
Froze our grip on the spades.
School-going wren boys and girls
Sporting mouth-organs and tin-whistles
Besieged the door of the house,
Shrilled their tunes as the frail sun
Fought its way into the freezing sky.
To the airs of 'The Wren' and 'Good King Wenceslaus'
and 'Silent Night'
We dallied, tucked away among the apple trees
Our ears cocked listening.

The sprawling fruit trees you planted
Half a century ago,
Fastened to their stakes with raffia,
Grew colder in the wind
As we killed the holiday
Tongueing the soil
With unmusical spades.
The wren's spring-drunk melody
Like a hot whiskey cheered us
While the apples tossed their branches
No more than a child stirs his sleeping limbs,
Caught us up in their moss-covered arms,
Dragged each closer to his own solitude.
Work had its own rhythm regardless.

A Drink of Spring, 1979

DECEMBER 1889: O'SHEA v. O'SHEA AND PARNELL

The *Evening News and Post,* a Tory sheet, published on Saturday a
statement to the effect that William Henry O'Shea, commonly called
Captain O'Shea, of 124 Victoria Street, Westminster, and J.P. for the
county Clare, had instituted a suit for divorce against his wife, Katherine
(to whom he is married for nearly a quarter of a century), sister of the
distinguished soldier, Sir Evelyn Wood, and aunt to the present Sir
Matthew Wood, Baronet, and had named Mr Parnell as co-respondent.

The *Evening News* was the first publication to give currency to the
statement, which afterwards became the common property of the news
agencies. But the *Evening News* did more. It published what purports to
be an interview with O'Shea in his chambers. The 'interview' is worked
up in the stereotyped fashion. O'Shea's 'cosy breakfast room' is the
scene. O'Shea's son is introduced. O'Shea offers the reporter the
friendly cigarette. They have a most delicate subject, and the injured
O'Shea effusively expresses his gratitude to the 'Editor' for sending his
representative to inquire into his domestic affairs. After telling the
reporter that it was true that he had filed his petition and had named Mr
Parnell as co-respondent, 'but how the deuce did you hear of it?' asked
the Captain. The reticent representative did 'not explain'. And, instead
of answering, he put a very pertinent question – for we must not call
anything this most insinuating of interviewers did on this interesting
occasion impertinent, immediately afterwards.

'Is it also true,' he asked, 'that you do not claim damages?' 'Of course I
do not,' is the reply. Why the 'of course' this precious 'interview' does
not elucidate. And so the pair parted with mutual courtesies.

Now, it is a curious fact that not very long ago the *Evening News*, which seems to be so entirely *en rapport* with Captain O'Shea, was obliged to make a public apology to Mr Parnell for linking his name with that of Mrs O'Shea in its columns in an unwarranted and unwarrantable way. It is the same paper which is again selected as the medium for Captain O'Shea's Christmas unbosoming of himself. The *Evening News* follows up the interview by a comment stating that 'amongst politicians' the affair was 'the one subject of discussion' and that 'speculation is not so much about the case proper as about the effect it may have on the political situation and the balance of parties.' And much more in this strain, the whole winding up with 'a telegram' from 'a Dublin correspondent' describing the 'sensation' here.

All this becomes very significant by the light of the gentlemanly and dignified statement which Mr Parnell promptly made to our London representative, and which he authorises us to publish today. Mr Parnell had not heard what the *Evening News* reporter was in such full possession of. He had not heard that proceedings had been taken by Captain O'Shea, but for the past three years, since Captain O'Shea had been separated from the Irish Parliamentary Party, he had been threatening the Irish Leader with such proceedings. Mr Parnell then adds that he has reliable information that Mr Edward Caulfield Houston, the hirer of Pigott, had been inciting O'Shea to take those proceedings. He has reliable information that the same Houston procured the writing of the libellous article already referred to in the *Evening News*, and that Houston had induced an American journalist named Ives to offer it to that sheet for publication. He believes that O'Shea was induced to take the proceedings by Houston in the interests of *The Times*, and that it is all done in the interest of *The Times* in view of the pending libel action by him against that paper, to be tried next month.

We do not touch upon the relations between the O'Sheas and Mr Parnell. That is their business. We will only say this, that the public have the utmost and the best proven confidence in what Mr Parnell says, and that they have no confidence at all in what O'Shea says. He swore as a witness for *The Times* before the Forgeries Commission that the Pigott signatures were Mr Parnell's. Mr Parnell endured the obloquy patiently, heroically. Providence could not have compensated this long-suffering gentleman by a more complete, a more striking, a more ample vindication. Every means that could be resorted to – libel, forgery, perjury, passion, prejudice – were pressed into the service by his enemies against him. He rose calmly triumphant above them all, and trampled them under foot as an archangel might stamp upon a many-headed dragon. But the assassins have plucked up courage for another stroke. Having failed to break the Irish Leader, and with him the Irish Party politically, they renew the attempt on a new line, and essay to stain him socially. No public man in ancient or modern times could have come through the cruel ordeal through which Mr Parnell has passed more unscathed, more pure. He stands before fair and honourable England a Bayard without fear and without reproach. And we believe that the sympathy of every honest man and woman, from John o' Groat's to Land's End, will be with him, and against the vile conspirators who still beset his path. . .

The Freeman's Journal, December 30 1889

A DUBLIN CHRISTMAS

Christy Brown

Too soon they came for him, chafing his limbs with rough gentleness to put warmth back into him, vastly unaware of that other warmth that shut out the real and more frightening cold, and with loud hurrahs and monkey tumblings in the snow they wheeled him down the brighter streets where the garish shop fronts threw yellow rectangles upon the glistening pavements; snowflakes swirled around the burning lamp-posts in a frenzy; all was noise, hurry, torrential footfalls murdering the snow, the mad, glad, spellbound faces staring into yawning glittering gaps of shop windows, snowflakes clinging to eyelashes, the rims of hats, the shoulders of heavy coats; girls shaking it from their pretty fur hoods, laughing up at the young men, who grinned and held the umbrellas higher in a protective, ostentatious way; people walking dream-like, with slow mesmerised steps, men's pipes glowing in the hard air, smell of tobacco pungent, pleasurable; portly red-faced dealers with push-car stalls trundling through the teeming thoroughfares with lusty, gusty cries of brash bantering wrangling and wheedling; a paper-boy with broken shoes and no socks, pinched monkey face grinning expectantly, thin flinty old-before-its-time voice speaking raucously, yelling out the names of the evening newspapers; a bus grinding to a stop, disgorging passengers, the impassive, remote faces of the people inside gazing ahead as if they had no existence or perceived no life except that inside their brightly-lit, enclosed, mobile world. The door of a public house across the street opened suddenly, shedding warm rich marmalade-streaks of light upon the mushy, slushy pavement, emitting a brief bombardment of bedlam sounds mysterious and enthralling to the boys who gathered outside waiting to wheedle money from their fathers, elder brothers or drunken strangers as they emerged from that pounding, resounding, smoke-filled, song-racked furnace of hard-faced, cement-booted working-men and beshawled, sharp-eyed, hair-loosened women smelling strangely of cabbage and cinnamon, with cheap little holly trees wrapped in red tissue paper stuck on tables, tinsel trampled underfoot, the gaudy parcels splashed and sploshed with brown spilled beer. A man hobbled out with a crooked shortened leg and a huge surgical boot; he careered wildly between rows of jeering boys, cursing and flailing with his fists; he fell and squirmed maddeningly in the snow as they roared and danced around him, prodding him with sticks and pelting him with hastily scooped-up snowballs, as he, with horribly contorted face and saliva-dripping mouth, tried to rise, his breathless baleful maledictions shooting out at them like bullets. A

woman, neither young nor old, stood scowling at a lane entrance, wearing a violent-coloured scarf, her skirt plastered against her thighs, lifting her face that glowed weirdly red in the neon light from the pub to men who passed, spitting and cursing after them as church bells tolled cleanly in the teeming air and a dog howled hungrily in the depths of the lane. The man at last found his feet and swung round on his tormentors, who scattered with wild jeers. The man stumbled and would have fallen again had not the woman by the lane come over and grabbed his arm, steadying him.

'A terrible way to treat a poor unfortunate man,' she screamed, 'and in the month of Christmas! God's curse on yous!'

Down All the Days, 1970

ESCAPE FROM INNISKILLEN

George Story

Towards the latter end of *December,* Major General *Mackarty* made his Escape from *Inniskillen,* who had remained there a Prisoner ever since the Rout at *Newtown-Butler;* he had been Sick, and at that time writ to Major General *Kirk* to get leave of the Duke to have his Guard removed, which he complained of was troublesome in his Sickness, this was done; but at his Recovery (they say) a Serjeant and some Men were put upon him again. The Town it seems stands upon a Lough, and the Water came to the Door of the House where he was confined, or very near it. He found means to corrupt a Serjeant, and so got two small Boats, called Cotts, to carry him and his best Moveables off in the Night. The Serjeant went along with him, but returned that Night to deliver a Letter, which, and *Mackarty's* Pass, being found in the Lining of his Hat, he was the next Day shot for it.

The General was much concerned when he heard of *Mackarty's* Escape, and said he took him to be a Man of Honour, but he would not expect that in an Irish-Man any more. Col. *Hamilton,* the Governour of *Inniskillin,* was blamed for his Negligence, but he came to *Lisburn* and desired a Tryal, which could not be, for want of Field-Officers, till the 15*th* of *March,* at what time he produced Major General *Kirk's* Letter to him, by which he was cleared.

About *Christmas* there happened an unlucky Accident at *Belfast;* *Cranmer, Bowls* and *Morley,* three Lieutenants in Major General *Kirk's* Regiment, happened to kill two Masters of Ships, and being tryed by a Court-Marshal, the thing appeared so ill, that they were all three shot.

A True and Impartial History of the Most Material Occurrences in the Kingdom of Ireland During the Last Two Years, 1691

A CHRISTMAS TOAST.

HERE'S TO THE HOUSE THIS CHRISTMAS NIGHT
TO THE GOOD WOMAN, HER STORE AND FLOCK,
WHO MAKES THE FIRE AND CANDLE BRIGHT
FOR HOMELESS FOLK.

UNTO THAT HOUSE AND THE WARM FIRE,
AND TO THE BED AND TO THE FEAST
THERE SHALL COME IN THE WORLD'S DESIRE —
THE LITTLEST.

THE LITTLEST LIKE AN UNFLEDGED BIRD
SHALL COME TO HIS STARVED WORLD AGAIN
AND WHERE LOVE SPREADS THE FEAST, THE
WORD
SHALL BE WITH MEN.

KATHARINE TYNAN.

130

THE WREN HUNT

Anne O'Dowd and Mairead Reynolds

The Wren Hunt is one of the most elaborate of bird rituals surviving in Europe, being preserved in England, Scotland, Wales, the Isle of Man, France, but perhaps more vigorously in Ireland than elsewhere.

In Ireland St Stephen's Day was the day on which the Wren Boys did their rounds. This was and to a certain extent is still a custom in the provinces of Munster, Leinster and Connacht. It is interesting in this respect to note that the custom is virtually absent from an area co-extensive with the old province of Ulster, an area which comprises the counties of Armagh, Antrim, Derry, Donegal, Down and the northern half of counties Louth and Fermanagh. In many areas the wren was borne on a bush of holly or ivy decorated with brightly coloured papers, on a pole or on sticks shaped to form a cross. In other districts it was carried in some small container such as a hollow turnip or in a mock bier such as the Wren Box from County Galway. Where the killing of the wren was disapproved of in recent years, toy birds or a potato, with feathers tucked on it to represent a wren, were substituted. The carcass of the wren is thrown away in the evening, but in certain areas the wren is buried in front of a house where no welcome was given to the procession. There is one County Clare record of the wren being interred as a mark of honour at the house where the Wren Boys were best treated.

Parties of Wren Boys vary in number, generally about four to ten members, but often there might be as few as two or as many as twenty. Those who wish to go on the wren visit make specially decorated dresses and, singing, dancing and playing music, they visit each house in the area and ask for a small contribution to help bury the wren. The musical instruments played by the Wren Boys include fiddle, melodeon and mouth organ. Special tambourines were often made for the occasion. These were made from hoops of wood covered tightly with goat-skin. Pieces of tin were sometimes tacked loosely on the hoop so that they jingled when the tambourine was beaten.

The song sung or chanted by the Wren Boys varies in different localities but all recorded versions are disjointed. . .

The two examples of the song printed below give the general content. The first version, it will be noted, leaves spaces to include personal names and place-names of the localities to which the Wren Boys made their visit:

Mr. . . is a worthy man
And to his house we brought the wran;
The wran, the wran as you may see,
Is guarded upon a holly tree,
A bunch of ribbons by his side
And the . . . boys to be his bride.
Although he's small his family's great,
Rise up, good people, and give us a treat.
    Hurrah me boys! hurrah!

Oh, Droleen, Droleen, where's your nest?
It's in the wood that I love best,
Under the holly and ivy tree,
Where the . . . boys came hunting me.
The Wran, the Wran, the king of all birds.
St Stephen's morn was caught in the furze.
We hunted him up and we hunted him down
And in the wood we knocked him down.

132

On Christmas day I turned the spit,
I burned my finger and feel it yet,
Between my finger and my thumb
Came a blister as big as a plum.
I have a small box under my arm,
A few pence will do it no harm,
And if you fill it of the best
I hope in heaven your soul will rest.
But if you fill it of the small
It won't agree with the Wran Boys at all.
So, up with the kettle and down with the pan;
Give us your answer and let us be gone.
    Hurrah, me boys! Hurrah![1]

The first two lines of the third verse seem to bear no relation to either the previous two verses or the remainder of the third. However, some meaning may be found for this obscure reference in the following belief recorded by T. Lupton in the sixteenth century.

'It is much to be marvelled at the little bird called a wren, being fastened to a stick of hazel newly gathered, doth turn about and roast itself.'[2]

The second version was recorded in County Mayo in 1936:

Dreóilín, Dreóilín, righ na n-éan,
Is mór do mhuirghín is is beag tú h-éin;
Éirí suas, a bhean a'tighe,
Agus béir ar chois na sginne bidhe.
Tabhair a chuid h-éin do'n dreóilín
Agus nár chráidh Dia do chroidhe.[3]

Traditional explanations as to the origin of the Wren Hunt are consistent with the occurrence of the custom only in the predominantly Catholic areas of Ireland. These explanations refer to the wren betraying the Irish by alarming the armies of King William on one occasion and of Cromwell on another. Other explanations refer to an earlier period of the Danes in Ireland: '. . . the Irish on a certain occasion had planned a night attack on their camp; they were silently creeping forward and had, unperceived by the Danes' sentries, reached to almost charging distance when a flock of "scoot-wrens", which had been disturbed and had flown on in front of them, lit on some drums near the sentries, who were asleep, and by their titters of alarm and their hopping about, awoke the sentries, who perceived their danger and so aroused the camp to drive off the Irish with heavy loss'.[4] Other explanations of the custom refer to the betrayal by the wren of both St Stephen and Our Lord.

However, none of these explanations is entirely satisfactory and it appears that we have a custom of which, being quite ancient, the true meaning and significance have been forgotten.

In the counties of Cork and Kerry, but more especially in the latter, about Tralee and in the Dingle Peninsula, the Wren Boys usually had a *Láir Bhán* (White Mare). . . This consists of a rectangular frame covered by a white sheet and a carved wooden horse-head and dangling feet. The lower jaw, which is movable, is worked by a string by the operator concealed beneath the sheet.

The origin of the custom of the *Láir Bhán* is not certain. Indeed, the *Láir Bhán* procession is closely related to that of the *Mari Lwyd* (Grey Mare) in Wales and *Laare Van* (White Mare) in the Isle of Man. The *Mari Lwyd* custom has been described as 'a pre-Christian horse ceremony which may be associated with similar customs spread over many parts of the world'. It is plausible, as with the origin of the Wren Hunt, that the original symbolic meaning of the *Láir Bhán* has been lost but that it was retained as a traditional custom and became a major part of the Wren Boy procession in certain areas at Christmastime.

However, the *Láir Bhán* may originally have been used more frequently than on the one occasion at Christmas. A record of the custom, written 125 years ago at Ballycotton, County Cork, refers to the *Láir Bhán* playing a role in Hallowe'en festivities: 'On Samhain's Eve, 31 October, a rustic procession perambulated the district between Ballycotton and Trabolgan, along the coast. The parties represented themselves as messengers of the Muck Olla, in whose name they levied contributions on farmers; as usual they were accompanied by sundry youths, sounding lustily on cows' horns; at the end of the procession was a figure enveloped in a white robe or sheet, having, as it were, the head of a mare; this personage was called the *Láir Bhán*.[5]

The fantastic costume worn by the Wren Boys can be looked on as no more than a disguise, 'the continuation of an immemorial ritual practice, a link between the civic, courtly and collegiate disguisings known to history and the pagan survivals. . . which here and there linger into the present time',[6] and the purpose of which is always the same: to conceal identity.

The type of garments worn by Wren Boys in modern times has become increasingly uniform and an almost military-like costume has been adopted. However, from available records of Wren Boy costume, there is a definite implication that straw was an early if not original material.[7] The change to the later type of costume possibly occurred as a natural development. Straw is an unmanageable material for most people and, unless taught the art by some skilled person, it was far easier to substitute with purchasable goods and personal and household items.

Records from Roscommon and Kerry give elaborate accounts of a complex ceremony, and appear to illustrate facets of Wren Hunt custom intertwined with those of the folk play – the Mummers and Christmas Rhymers. One account from County Roscommon reads:

'The leader is dressed up in a covering of straw tied around him and has his face blackened. He carries a big staff to which the wren is tied. . . One is dressed in women's clothes, the rest have scarves and ribbons tied to their sleeves and any sort of fanciful headgear. . . The leader goes first and jumps about; the rest dance.'[8]

The second record from Dingle, County Kerry, is probably the most elaborate account of wren ritual in Ireland and refers to a period towards the end of the nineteenth century. 'Up to 35 men took part, some carrying wooden swords, others wielding a fool's bladder on a stick, wearing suits of straw or described as women. These were called *oinsigh* – women fools. The party carried banners and poles, the bearers being decked with ribbons in the same style as the Mummers of the folk play. The "Captain" wore an old-style green uniform and carried a sword. The Wren Man, who carried a dead wren in a holly bush fastened to a pole, also wore a special costume. A mock battle was staged between those bearing swords, the Fools and the strawboys with bladders.'[9]

NOTES

[1]Department of Irish Folklore (University College, Dublin) Collections, MS 972, p.253.

[2]T. Lupton, *A Thousand Notable Things*, etc. London, 1595. Quoted in Armstrong, E.A., *The Folklore of Birds*, 2nd edition, New York, 1970, p.176.

[3]Department of Irish Folklore (University College, Dublin) Collections, MS 191, p.231.

[4]'Omurethi', 'Customs Peculiar to Certain Days Formerly observed in Co. Kildare' in *Journal Kildare Archaeological Society*, 5, pp.452–3.

[5]W. Hackett, 'Porcine Legends' in *Transactions of the Kilkenny Archaeological Society*, 11, 1852–3, pp.308–9. Quoted in I.C. Peate 'Mari Lwyd – Láir Bháin' in *Folklife*, 1, 1963, p.95.

[6]Margaret Dean-Smith, 'Disguise in English Folk Drama', *Folklife* 1, 1963, p.97.

[7]Alan Gailey, 'Straw Costume in Irish Folk Customs' *Folklife* 6, 1968, pp.83–93.

[8]Ibid. This quotation originally comes from *Folk-Lore* 18, 1907, p.439.

[9]E.A. Armstrong, op. cit., reference 2, p.157.

Christmas and the Children, 1976

CHRISTMAS AND PANTOS

Paddy Crosbie

Christmas in Dublin was Christmas no matter what trouble or war was on. During the very poor period up to about 1920, toys were very scarce in all homes. Rag dolls, many of them home-made, and wooden toys like engines, were the usual ones for girls and boys respectively. Stockings were hung up, however, on Christmas Eve, no matter how bleak the outlook.

I got a Meccano set, No. 1A, in 1920 that I cherished and kept intact for years. Mona got her first real doll the same year, one with a smooth rosy face and a head of hair. The body was just rag and sawdust. When Mossy and I were altar-boys, Christmas morning was a very busy one as each priest 'said' three Masses. But there was electricity in the air.

The days before Christmas were full of magic. Woolworths, 'the 3d. and 6d. store', was a fairyland to all children, and unknown to our parents we – some of the gang and myself – often sneaked down town to wander up and down through the counters in Woolworth's store. We eyed the toys enviously – most of them were German made – and dreamed of stockings full to the top with the toys on show. We paid visits also to a small Bazaar on the other side of Henry Street. There were no fairy lights strung across the street, but the well-lit windows of every shop in Henry Street and Mary Street satisfied us to the full.

Whenever my mother brought the three of us down town, we visited Todd Burns, the Henry Street Warehouse (now Roches Stores), Arnotts, Brown Thomas and Clerys. She only did this when she had something definite in mind, usually a pair of shoes. She made most of the clothes we wore and often, in my bed, I could hear the whirr of the old Singer sewing machine which she pedalled in spasms to complete a pair of trousers, or a jacket, for Mossy or myself.

To us, Moore Street was the heart of Christmas. My father loved to bring us with him through the Christmas throngs and listen to the wit and sarcasm of the hawkers:

'Listen ma'am, if you're not buying, I'll trouble you to stop maulin' that turkey.'

'I have a right to feel the goods, before I decide to buy.'

'Hey, Julia, come over here and listen to this oul' wan. There's chokes-off being gev by her ladyship.'

As I let my mind wander back to the Christmases of long ago I find myself listing the well known shops of the period. I remember Hopkins & Hopkins, Elverys, Lemons, McDowells, Findlaters, the Carlisle Building, the name of Albert Coates the piano tuner – all of them in O'Connell Street. In Capel Street, there were Baxendales, McQuillans and Kearneys. In Henry Street, besides the Henry Street Warehouse, there were Todd Burns, Liptons, and the Fifty Shilling Tailors. Atkinson's Poplin and Walpole's Irish Linen also come to mind. And from the grown-ups we heard:

'Are yeh goin' home for Christmas?'

'No, I'm sendin' a pound instead.'

I can't remember Santa Clauses in the shops in those early days. Maybe they were there, but I don't remember being brought to see one. One thing I can remember clearly is the three consecutive Christmas Eves when my father came home drunk with the same friend, Paul Butterly, each carrying a large turkey. On the three occasions my father did the very same thing – he got sick and then fell asleep on the sofa in the kitchen. He never smoked and took only the odd drink during the year, but Christmas Eve bowled him over.

Christmas Day in the parlour was a completely family day. Mossy, Mona and I played with our toys, the ones we had got in our stockings. We always played cards, games like Snap, and sometimes Pontoon. My father sang at the piano too, and this was when my mother showed her harmonising talent. Mossy and Mona were having music lessons from Aggie Quinn, and they played from their repertoire. I shall remember always the cosy comfortable feeling of those Christmas Days near the fire in our parlour. The feeling seemed to fade as I grew older, and I recall actually wishing it to remain. Christmas, however, was never Christmas without the Pantomime.

> Yez can keep your cowboy pictures,
> I can see them any day;
> I could do without me comic cuts
> Or a jaunt on Markey's dray.
> But there's one thing that I'd hate to miss,
> If I did, I'd feel, well, queer,
> It's when me father brings the family
> To the Pantomine each year.

The Pantomimes were to be seen in all of the theatres except the Theatre Royal. Our regular theatre was the Olympia, but we were brought also to the Tivoli and the Queens. In our own area, a Christmas Panto was presented annually in the Father Mathew Hall in Church Street, and I remember going on three occasions with a crowd of boys to the Boys' Brigade Hall in Lower Church Street, near the old church of St Michan's. The favourite panto was *Cinderella*.

Outside of the city theatres were to be found young hawkers with leaflets, which they waved as they shouted 'Pantomine Songs a Penny, Pantomine Songs a Penny.' And every year without fail came the fellow with the peaked cap who sang 'One of the Old Reserves' to the queues. The fellow who sang this song sometimes changed it to 'The Wreck of the Bugaboo', which was the story of a shipwreck or bargewreck on the Grand Canal. I had heard him so often at the other theatre queues that I recall some of the lines:

> Come all you gentle hearted lads and listen unto me,
> I'll tell of my adventures upon the briny sea,
> Of the hardships and the dangers, the ones that I went through
> When I shipped as cook and steward on board the Bugaboo.

The barrel-organ also made its appearance at the Pantomime queues and there was another regular with a mouth-organ who never played any tune but the one – 'Show me the Way to go Home'. But the waiting seemed an eternity.

> At last the doors are opened,
> Me father pays for all,
> He takes young Gaby in his arms,
> An' up the steps we crawl.
> It's an awful journey upwards,
> Though us kids go in 'leps',
> But me mudder pants an' me father laughs,
> An' he says, 'Gerrup them steps'.

At last we reach the gallery;
We rush down to the front,
Last year our Mossy slipped an' fell,
An' he got an awful dunt.
We sit down on our overcoats,
'Cause the seats are like cement,
An' then out loud we read and spell
Each big advertis'ment.

The conductor comes out smilin',
The lights do dim, then out,
The band strikes up a marchy tune,
An' someone starts to shout.
The curtain rises slowly,
We see a village green,
An' we all just sit there starin',
'Cause it's like a lovely dream.

One year there was a 'divil',
An' he used to disappear;
A hole used open in the floor –
It made hell seem awful near.
But the divil was fat and got stuck that night,
Though he tried to push and pull,
Then a voice from the gallery shouted out
'Three cheers, the place is full'.

Me mudder an' me father,
They love the Pantomime,
An' when the funny man appears,
They laugh at every line,
An' me mudder loves the music too,
An' when a man appears,
Who sings ould songs like 'Nellie Dean',
Her eyes fill up with tears.

The days after Christmas Day were happy days. Toys and dolls were brought out on the street to be boasted about:
    'What's that?'
    'A Meccano set. You can make hundreds of things with it.'
    'They're on'y bits of tin. My father can get plenty of them tings.'
    'What did you get?'
    'I gorra bike.'
    'Yeh bloody liar. Where is it?'

'Me mother wouldn't let me brin' it out.'
'Let's all go up to your house; we can see it there.'
'My mother's gone out.'
'Yeh didn't ger' an'tin' in your stockin'.'
'You're another, I did.'
'Here's Cocky! What did *you* get?'
'I gorra shillin' an an apple.'
'Tony gorra football – a real one.'
'Like one you have to pump up?'
'Yeh, one o' them. Let's ask Tony to come up to the Park. . .'

Your Dinner's Poured Out, 1981

CHRISTMAS AT RAVENSDALE, COUNTY LOUTH

Dr Wm Drennan

To Mrs M. McTier at Belfast

December 24 1799

I am tired of the Park here, with its root-house and moss-house and grotto and paltry cascade.

The face of nature is in this place beautiful and romantic, but the face of men is savage, dark and unhealthy. The women all witches, and the men seem all in premature old age. Confidence in society is absolutely lost, I believe, for ever, but there must be fidelity to each other in the lowest rank. The main coach was stopped a day or two ago at seven o'clock in the evening by a dozen men not half-a-mile from the barrack, where fifty men are quartered, and the mail-bag alone was taken, the passengers unmolested, and the robbers as *yet* remain undiscovered; but the consequence is that a dozen of the poor cottagers who were so unlucky as to live near the spot are sent to gaol, their labour lost, and their families frightened to death, though in some days they will be sent about their business without getting any sort of compensation. I saw a landlord the other day hunt an active old woman who was stealing some sticks from his hedge for a Christmas fire, but she got over a wall and threw him out; and the rector, who, when curate, was suspected to be an United man, boasted of the numbers he had taken in the mountains and lodged, first in his parlour and next in the prison. A collier was cast away on this shore. The poor country people came down in flocks, offering the same price as the great men for the coal, if allowed to take them in small quantities, but the gentlemen carted them, every particle, away, because they got them a shilling or two cheaper by the ton.

The Drennan Letters, 1931

THE MISSES MORKAN'S ANNUAL
CHRISTMAS SUPPER

James Joyce

On the landing outside the drawing-room Gabriel found his wife and Mary Jane trying to persuade Miss Ivors to stay for supper. But Miss Ivors, who had put on her hat and was buttoning her cloak, would not stay. She did not feel in the least hungry and she had already over-stayed her time.

'But only for ten minutes, Molly,' said Mrs Conroy. 'That won't delay you.'

'To take a pick itself,' said Mary Jane, 'after all your dancing.'

'I really couldn't,' said Miss Ivors.

'I am afraid you didn't enjoy yourself at all,' said Mary Jane hopelessly.

'Ever so much, I assure you,' said Miss Ivors, 'but you really must let me run off now.'

'But how can you get home?' asked Mrs Conroy.

'O, it's only two steps up the quay.'

Gabriel hesitated a moment and said:

'If you will allow me, Miss Ivors, I'll see you home if you are really obliged to go.'

But Miss Ivors broke away from them.

'I won't hear of it,' she cried. 'For goodness' sake go in to your suppers and don't mind me. I'm quite well able to take care of myself.'

'Well, you're the comical girl, Molly,' said Mrs Conroy frankly.

'*Beannacht libh,*' cried Miss Ivors, with a laugh, as she ran down the staircase.

Mary Jane gazed after her, a moody puzzled expression on her face, while Mrs Conroy leaned over the banisters to listen for the hall-door. Gabriel asked himself was he the cause of her abrupt departure. But she did not seem to be in ill humour: she had gone away laughing. He stared blankly down the staircase.

At the moment Aunt Kate came toddling out of the supper-room, almost wringing her hands in despair.

'Where is Gabriel?' she cried. 'Where on earth is Gabriel? There's everyone waiting in there, stage to let, and nobody to carve the goose!'

'Here I am, Aunt Kate!' cried Gabriel, with sudden animation, 'ready to carve a flock of geese, if necessary.'

A fat brown goose lay at one end of the table and at the other end, on a bed of creased paper strewn with sprigs of parsley, lay a great ham, stripped of its outer skin and peppered over with crust crumbs, a neat paper frill round its shin and beside this was a round of spiced beef. Between these rival ends ran parallel lines of side-dishes: two little minsters of jelly, red and yellow; a shallow dish full of blocks of blancmange and red jam, a large green leaf-shaped dish with a stalk-shaped handle, on which lay bunches of purple raisins and peeled almonds, a companion dish on which lay a solid rectangle of Smyrna figs, a dish of custard topped with grated nutmeg, a small bowl full of chocolates and sweets wrapped in gold and silver papers and a glass vase in which stood some tall celery stalks. In the centre of the table there stood, as sentries to a fruit-stand which upheld a pyramid of oranges and American apples, two squat old-fashioned decanters of cut glass, one containing port and the other dark sherry. On the closed square piano a pudding in a huge yellow dish lay in waiting and behind it were three squads of bottles of stout and ale and minerals, drawn up according to the colours of their uniforms, the first two black, with brown and red labels, the third and smallest squad white, with transverse green sashes.

Gabriel took his seat boldly at the head of the table and, having looked to the edge of the carver, plunged his fork firmly into the goose. He felt quite at ease now for he was an expert carver and liked nothing better than to find himself at the head of a well-laden table.

'Miss Furlong, what shall I send you?' he asked. 'A wing or a slice of the breast?'

'Just a small slice of the breast.'

'Miss Higgins, what for you?'

'O, anything at all, Mr Conroy.'

While Gabriel and Miss Daly exchanged plates of goose and plates of ham and spiced beef Lily went from guest to guest with a dish of hot floury potatoes wrapped in a white napkin. This was Mary Jane's idea and she had also suggested apple sauce for the goose but Aunt Kate had said that plain roast goose without any apple sauce had always been good enough for her and she hoped she might never eat worse. Mary Jane waited on her pupils and saw that they got the best slices and Aunt Kate and Aunt Julia opened and carried across from the piano bottles of stout and ale for the gentlemen and bottles of minerals for the ladies. There was a great deal of confusion and laughter and noise, the noise of orders and counter-orders, of knives and forks, of corks and glass-stoppers. Gabriel began to carve second helpings as soon as he had finished the first round without serving himself. Everyone protested loudly so that he compromised by taking a long draught of stout for he had found the carving hot work. Mary Jane settled down quietly to her supper but Aunt Kate and Aunt Julia were still toddling round the table, walking on each other's heels, getting in each other's way and giving each other unheeded orders. Mr Browne begged of them to sit down and eat their suppers and so did Gabriel but they said there was time enough, so that, at last, Freddy Malins stood up and, capturing Aunt Kate, plumped her down on her chair amid general laughter.

When everyone had been well served Gabriel said, smiling:

'Now, if anyone wants a little more of what vulgar people call stuffing let him or her speak.'

A chorus of voices invited him to begin his own supper and Lily came forward with three potatoes which she had reserved for him.

'Very well,' said Gabriel amiably, as he took another preparatory draught, 'kindly forget my existence, ladies and gentlemen, for a few minutes.'

He set to his supper and took no part in the conversation with which the table covered Lily's removal of the plates. The subject of talk was the opera company which was then at the Theatre Royal. Mr Bartell D'Arcy, the tenor, a dark-complexioned young man with a smart moustache, praised very highly the leading contralto of the company but Miss Furlong thought she had a rather vulgar style of production. Freddy Malins said there was a negro chieftain singing in the second part of the Gaiety pantomime who had one of the finest tenor voices he had ever heard.

'Have you heard him?' he asked Mr Bartell D'Arcy across the table.

'No,' answered Mr Bartell D'Arcy carelessly.

'Because,' Freddy Malins explained, 'now I'd be curious to hear your opinion of him. I think he has a grand voice.'

'It takes Teddy to find out the really good things,' said Mr Browne familiarly to the table.

'And why couldn't he have a voice too?' asked Freddy Malins sharply. 'Is it because he's only a black?'

Nobody answered this question and Mary Jane led the table back to the legitimate opera. One of her pupils had given her a pass for *Mignon*. Of course it was very fine, she said, but it made her think of poor Georgina Burns. Mr Browne could go back farther still, to the old Italian companies that used to come to Dublin – Tietjens, Ilma de Murzka, Campanini, the great Trebelli Giuglini, Ravelli, Aramburo. Those were the days, he said, when there was something like singing to be heard in Dublin. He told too of how the top gallery of the old Royal used to be packed night after night, of how one night an Italian tenor had sung five encores to 'Let me like a Soldier fall', introducing a high C every time, and of how the gallery boys would sometimes in their enthusiasm unyoke the horses from the carriage of some great *prima donna* and pull her themselves through the streets to her hotel. Why did they never play the grand old operas now, he asked, *Dinorah, Lucrezia Borgia?* Because they could not get the voices to sing them: that was why.

'O, well,' said Mr Bartell D'Arcy, 'I presume there are as good singers

144

today as there were then.'

'Where are they?' asked Mr Browne defiantly.

'In London, Paris, Milan,' said Mr Bartell D'Arcy warmly. 'I suppose Caruso, for example, is quite as good, if not better than any of the men you have mentioned.'

'Maybe so,' said Mr Browne. 'But I may tell you I doubt it strongly.'

'O, I'd give anything to hear Caruso sing,' said Mary Jane.

'For me,' said Aunt Kate, who had been picking a bone, 'there was only one tenor. To please me, I mean. But I suppose none of you ever heard of him.'

'Who was he, Miss Morkan?' asked Mr Bartell D'Arcy politely.

'His name,' said Aunt Kate, 'was Parkinson. I heard him when he was in his prime and I think he had then the purest tenor voice that was ever put into a man's throat.'

'Strange,' said Mr Bartell D'Arcy. 'I never even heard of him.'

'Yes, yes, Miss Morkan is right,' said Mr Browne. 'I remember hearing of old Parkinson but he's too far back for me.'

'A beautiful, pure, sweet, mellow English tenor,' said Aunt Kate with enthusiasm.

Gabriel having finished, the huge pudding was transferred to the table. The clatter of forks and spoons began again. Gabriel's wife served out spoonfuls of the pudding and passed the plates down the table. Midway down they were held up by Mary Jane, who replenished them with raspberry or orange jelly or with blancmange and jam. The pudding was of Aunt Julia's making and she received praises for it from all quarters. She herself said that it was not quite brown enough.

'Well, I hope, Miss Morkan,' said Mr Browne, 'that I'm brown enough for you because, you know, I'm all brown.'

All the gentlemen, except Gabriel, ate some of the pudding out of compliment to Aunt Julia. As Gabriel never ate sweets the celery had been left for him. Freddy Malins also took a stalk of celery and ate it with his pudding. He had been told that celery was a capital thing for the blood and he was just then under doctor's care. Mrs Malins, who had been silent all through the supper, said that her son was going down to Mount Melleray in a week or so. The table then spoke of Mount Melleray, how bracing the air was down there, how hospitable the monks were and how they never asked for a penny-piece from their guests.

'And do you mean to say,' asked Mr Browne incredulously, 'that a chap can go down there and put up there as if it were a hotel and live on the fat of the land and then come away without paying anything?'

'O, most people give some donation to the monastery when they leave,' said Mary Jane.

'I wish we had an institution like that in our Church,' said Mr Browne candidly.

He was astonished to hear that the monks never spoke, got up at two in the morning and slept in their coffins. He asked what they did it for.

'That's the rule of the order,' said Aunt Kate firmly.

'Yes, but why?' asked Mr Browne.

Aunt Kate repeated that it was the rule, that was all. Mr Browne still seemed not to understand. Freddy Malins explained to him, as best he could, that the monks were trying to make up for the sins committed by all the sinners in the outside world. The explanation was not very clear for Mr Browne grinned and said:

'I like that idea very much but wouldn't a comfortable spring bed do them as well as a coffin?'

'The coffin,' said Mary Jane, 'is to remind them of their last end.'

As the subject had grown lugubrious it was buried in a silence of the table during which Mrs Malins could be heard saying to her neighbour in an indistinct undertone:

'They are very good men, the monks, very pious men.'

The raisins and almonds and figs and apples and oranges and chocolates and sweets were now passed about the table and Aunt Julia invited all the guests to have either port or sherry. At first Mr Bartell D'Arcy refused to take either but one of his neighbours nudged him and whispered something to him upon which he allowed his glass to be filled. Gradually as the last glasses were being filled the conversation ceased. A pause followed, broken only by the noise of the wine and by unsettlings of chairs. The Misses Morkan, all three, looked down at the tablecloth. Someone coughed once or twice and then a few gentlemen patted the table gently as a signal for silence. The silence came and Gabriel pushed back his chair and stood up.

The patting at once grew louder in encouragement and then ceased altogether. Gabriel leaned his ten trembling fingers on the tablecloth and smiled nervously at the company. Meeting a row of upturned faces he raised his eyes to the chandelier. The piano was playing a waltz tune and he could hear the skirts sweeping against the drawing-room door. People, perhaps, were standing in the snow on the quay outside, gazing up at the lighted windows and listening to the waltz music. The air was pure there. In the distance lay the park where the trees were weighted with snow. The Wellington Monument wore a gleaming cap of snow that flashed westward over the white field of Fifteen Acres.

He began:

'Ladies and Gentlemen, It has fallen to my lot this evening, as in years past, to perform a very pleasing task but a task for which I am afraid my poor powers as a speaker are all too inadequate.'

'No, no!' said Mr Browne.

'But, however that may be, I can only ask you tonight to take the will for the deed and to lend me your attention for a few moments while I

146

endeavour to express to you in words what my feelings are on this occasion.

'Ladies and Gentlemen, it is not the first time that we have gathered together under this hospitable roof, around this hospitable board. It is not the first time that we have been the recipients – or perhaps, I had better say, the victims – of the hospitality of certain good ladies.'

He made a circle in the air with his arm and paused. Everyone laughed or smiled at Aunt Kate and Aunt Julia and Mary Jane who all turned crimson with pleasure. Gabriel went on more boldly:

'I feel more strongly with every recurring year that our country has no tradition which does it so much honour and which it should guard so jealously as that of its hospitality. It is a tradition that is unique as far as my experience goes (and I have visited not a few places abroad) among the modern nations. Some would say, perhaps, that with us it is rather a failing than anything to be boasted of. But granted even that, it is, to my mind, a princely failing, and one that I trust will long be cultivated among us. Of one thing, at least, I am sure. As long as this one roof shelters the good ladies aforesaid – and I wish from my heart it may do so for many and many a long year to come – the tradition of genuine warm-hearted courteous Irish hospitality, which our forefathers have handed down to us and which we in turn must hand down to our descendants, is still alive among us.'

A hearty murmur of assent ran round the table. It shot through Gabriel's mind that Miss Ivors was not there and that she had gone away discourteously: and he said with confidence in himself:

'Ladies and Gentlemen, a new generation is growing up in our midst, a generation actuated by new ideas and new principles. It is serious and enthusiastic for these new ideas and its enthusiasm, even when it is misdirected, is, I believe, in the main sincere. But we are living in a sceptical and, if I may use the phrase, a thought-tormented age: and sometimes I fear that this new generation, educated or hypereducated as it is, will lack those qualities of humanity, of hospitality, of kindly humour which belonged to an older day. Listening tonight to the names of all those great singers of the past it seemed to me, I must confess, that we were living in a less spacious age. Those days might, without exaggeration, be called spacious days: and if they are gone beyond recall let us hope, at least, that in gatherings such as this we shall still speak of them with pride and affection, still cherish in our hearts the memory of those dead and gone great ones whose fame the world will not willingly let die.'

'Hear, hear,' said Mr Browne loudly.

'But yet,' continued Gabriel, his voice falling into a softer inflection, 'there are always in gatherings such as this sadder thoughts that will recur to our minds: thoughts of the past, of youth, of changes, of absent faces that we miss here tonight. Our path through life is strewn with many such sad memories: and were we to brood upon them always we could not find the heart to go on bravely with our work among the living. We have all of us living duties and living affections which claim, and rightly claim, our strenuous endeavours.

'Therefore, I will not linger on the past. I will not let any gloomy moralising intrude upon us here tonight. Here we are gathered together for a brief moment from the bustle and rush of our everyday routine. We are met here as friends, in the spirit of good-fellowship, as colleagues, also to a certain extent, in the true spirit of *camaraderie*, and as the guests of – what shall I call them? – the Three Graces of the Dublin musical world.'

The table burst into applause and laughter at this allusion. Aunt Julia vainly asked each of her neighbours in turn to tell her what Gabriel had said.

'He says we are the Three Graces, Aunt Julia,' said Mary Jane.

Aunt Julia did not understand but she looked up, smiling, at Gabriel, who continued in the same vein:

'Ladies and Gentlemen, I will not attempt to play tonight the part that Paris played on another occasion. I will not attempt to choose between them. The task would be an invidious one and one beyond my poor powers. For when I view them in turn, whether it be our chief hostess herself, whose good heart, whose too good heart, has become a byword with all who know her, or her sister, who seems to be gifted with perennial youth and whose singing must have been a surprise and a revelation to us all tonight, or, last but not least, when I consider our youngest hostess, talented, cheerful, hard-working and the best of nieces, I confess, Ladies and Gentlemen, that I do not know to which of them I should award the prize.'

Gabriel glanced down at his aunts and, seeing the large smile on Aunt Julia's face and the tears which had risen to Aunt Kate's eyes, hastened to his close. He raised his glass of port gallantly, while every member of the company fingered a glass expectantly, and said loudly:

'Let us toast them all three together. Let us drink to their health, wealth, long life, happiness and prosperity and may they long continue to hold the proud and self-won position which they hold in their profession and the position of honour and affection which they hold in our hearts.'

All the guests stood up, glass in hand, and turning towards the three seated ladies, sang in unison, with Mr Browne as leader:

For they are jolly gay fellows,
For they are jolly gay fellows,
For they are jolly gay fellows,
Which nobody can deny.

148

Aunt Kate was making frank use of her handkerchief and even Aunt Julia seemed moved. Freddy Malins beat time with his pudding-fork and the singers turned towards one another, as if in melodious conference, while they sang with emphasis:

Unless he tells a lie,
Unless he tells a lie,

Then, turning once more towards their hostesses, they sang:

For they are jolly gay fellows,
For they are jolly gay fellows,
For they are jolly gay fellows,
Which nobody can deny.

The acclamation which followed was taken up beyond the door of the supper-room by many of the other guests and renewed time after time, Freddy Malins acting as officer with his fork on high.

The Dead, 1914

BUYING A GOOSE

J.B. Keane

Before Christmas I successfully engaged two geese. If you're ever taken down in the purchase of a goose, that is to say if you buy an old goose instead of a green one, you will not engage geese hastily nor will you buy at random from any Tom, Dick or Harry. To be quite candid I would put the same amount of preparation and planning into the purchase of a goose as I would into the robbing of a bank. Too many times in the past I was taken down in the matter of geese by otherwise honest people. In the country it is not considered a dishonest act to sell old geese to townies. Old geese must be sold to somebody and who better than townies. Few townies know the identities or dwelling places of goose producers so the disposer is nearly always safe from retaliation. In addition nearly all goose producers look alike, especially those who foist off ancient birds on the unwary and the unsuspecting.

You will always find them in the corner of the market where the ass and pony rails are thickest and they will always call you 'Sir' which, in my humble estimation, is the true hallmark of a scoundrel.

Luckily for me I have considerable experience in the engaging of geese. At the tender age of thirteen I was dispatched to the marketplace in Listowel having been commissioned to invest in a prime goose by an elderly neighbour. It was foolishly presumed at the time that I was a crafty young chap who would be more than a match for the wiles of dealers anxious to dispose of old geese.

Earlier that morning I was instructed in the ways of geese. Old geese were listless. Their eyes were lacklustre. Their beaks were more worn and of a darker yellow than those of young geese. Their laipeens were wrinkled and coarse. These were but a few of the many characteristics attached to geese and ganders of advanced years which were conveyed to me that morning by the pair who commissioned me to transact the purchase.

Armed with this vast array of knowledge and clutching two florins in my trouser pocket I entered the market. Great was the clamour of geese and turkeys not to mention ducks and drakes and hens and chickens. Ass and pony rails cluttered the scene. Everywhere bargains were being struck and satisfied customers departing with cross-winged braces of prime fowl grasped in either hand. I hardly knew where to begin. I looked in wonder at the great array of transports and countryfolk.

'Ah,' said a friendly voice behind me, 'is that yourself.' I barely recognised the visage of the man who addressed me. I knew him and yet I didn't know him. He had a friendly face, the sort you could im-

mediately trust. He knew my name although I couldn't tell his.

'I bet I know what you're looking for,' he said. 'I bet you're after a turkey for your mother.'

'No.' I said, 'I'm after a goose for oul' Mague Sullivan.'

'If you are,' said he, 'you'd better draw away from here', and he winked in the most conspiratorial way possible. I followed him past rails of gobbling turkeys, madly quacking ducks and hissing ganders. 'Half of these,' my new-found friend announced indicating the proprietors of the fowl all about us, 'would pick the eye out of your head or,' said he in a whisper, 'if you was gom enough to stick out your tongue that's the very last you'd see of it.'

He stopped at a corner of the market where an old shawled woman with a wrinkled face was attending to an ass rail of geese. She had, I recall to this very day, the kindliest and homeliest face one could wish to see. Her voice was soft and sweet and as near to Gaelic in sound and rhythm as English could be. More to the point she had geese for sale. My friend explained my predicament, how my purchasing power was restricted to four shillings and how I had been warned about dishonest people who would think nothing of fobbing off an elderly goose on an innocent person.

'Oh, *mo creach agus no leir,*' said the old woman to the heavens, 'may God in his mercy preserve us all, the young as well as the old, from them that would wrong innocent people.'

151

She made the sign of the cross after this aspiration and went, as she said herself, for to capture the tenderest goose in her rail.

'This is a fine sensible fellow here,' said she lifting up a chesty specimen for my approval.

'I declare to God,' said my friend, 'but that's as noble a young gander as I seen in sixty years, man and boy. Pay down your money quick, don't let someone else come and sweep him on you.'

I could not find the four shillings quickly enough. I handed it over and was given in return the bird which had so recently been exhibited. Proudly I hurried back to the house of Mague Sullivan.

'M'anam an diabhal,' said she when she beheld the gander, 'he's like he'd be the one age with myself.'

Stories from a Kerry Fireside, 1980

THE SECOND COMING

W.B. Yeats

Turning and turning in the widening gyre
The falcon cannot hear the falconer;
Things fall apart; the centre cannot hold;
Mere anarchy is loosed upon the world,
The blood-dimmed tide is loosed, and everywhere
The ceremony of innocence is drowned;
The best lack all conviction, while the worst
Are full of passionate intensity.

Surely some revelation is at hand;
Surely the Second Coming is at hand.
The Second Coming! Hardly are those words out
When a vast image out of *Spiritus Mundi*
Troubles my sight: somewhere in sands of the desert
A shape with lion body and the head of a man,
A gaze blank and pitiless as the sun,
Is moving its slow thighs, while all about it
Reel shadows of the indignant desert birds.
The darkness drops again; but now I know
That twenty centuries of stony sleep
Were vexed to nightmare by a rocking cradle,
And what rough beast, its hour come round at last,
Slouches towards Bethlehem to be born?

Michael Robartes and the Dancer, 1921

E.C.B

Rake down the fire
This Christmas Eve——
Over the fire seed
The ashes leave——

Three will stand by the fire
When the hearth is clean;
The Mother, the Son on each side
And Saint Bridget between.

Padraic Colum.

TRAGEDY AT CHRISTMAS

Robert Lloyd Praeger

It was on peat-covered hills near Gneevgullia, out to the north-east of Killarney, that there occurred, [around] the Christmas of 1896, an extensive bog-burst that attracted much attention on account of the tragic circumstances accompanying it, a family of eight persons, their home, and their livestock, having been carried away and buried. These bog-bursts or bog-slides are not very uncommon in Ireland, on account of the great prevalence of peat-bogs in the country. In certain conditions, the lower layers of a bog may become so highly charged with water that under the pressure of the superincumbent mass they gush out at the lowest point of the floor, dragging the wreck of the more solid upper layers after them. If the bog be large and deep, a great flood of semi-liquid matter may be ejected: and should the slope below the point of ejection be steep, a devastating torrent may result.

Unwise turf-cutting, by producing a high face without due preliminary draining, has been frequently the cause of these accidents. It was so in the fatal Kerry case; the face of the turf-cutting gave way, and a vast mass of peat and water precipitated itself down the valley, the flood ceasing only when it entered the lower Lake of Killarney, fourteen miles distant. When the flow finally died down, about a week after the outburst, a great saucer-shaped depression, at its deepest no less than forty-five feet below the former slightly convex surface, showed the amount of the extruded material. This, with the abundant stumps of pine which it had contained, was spread for miles over the lands below, the width of the covering varying according to the slope of the valley sides. 'The flood has left behind it, in the upper portion of the valley,' says a comtemporary account, 'a deposit of peat averaging three feet in thickness, here as everywhere contrasted by its black colour with the grassland or other surface on which it rests. Its compact convex margin, like that of outpoured oatmeal porridge, often two feet in height, serves equally well to define it; so that it was an easy task to determine and map the high-water level of the flood. The surface of the deposit was everywhere broken by great roots and trunks of Scotch fir, which, in their enormous numbers, bore convincing testimony to the evisceration which the bog had undergone. The appearance of this sea of black peat, with its protruding stumps of black trees, was a sight melancholy in the extreme.'*

The evacuated area showed a depression three-quarters of a mile long and broad; the upper crust had broken away along a series of concentric cracks as the lower layers rushed out, and thousands of floes a yard or more thick went careering down the valley, to be stranded here and there; the centre of the area of movement was swept bare down to the gravelly drift on which the bog had rested; near the edges, the heather-covered floes still lay about, getting more numerous and closer together till the margin of the firm bog was reached, where the cracks could be seen in all incipient stages. I had ample opportunities for studying this disastrous bog-burst, for I was one of a small party, headed by W.J. Sollas, who a few days after the occurrence hurried down from Dublin to investigate on behalf of the Royal Dublin Society. It was dark cold weather, the Reeks were white with snow, the district a rather desolate one, and I well remember the feeling of depression with which we gazed at that black slimy mass stretching down the valley, somewhere in which lay entombed the bodies of Cornelius Donnelly, his wife, and his six children. Other bog-bursts, old and recent, I have visited, but none so devastating as that of Knocknageeha.

NOTE
*R.L. Praeger and W.J. Sollas, *Report of the Committee. . . to investigate the recent Bog-flow in Kerry*, Sci. Proc. Royal Dublin Soc., N.S., vol. viii, pp. 475–508, plates 17–19. 1897.

The Way that I Went, 1937

THE CHRISTMAS PUDDING

Katharine Tynan

My poor dear sister had addressed herself to the hopeless task of making a housewife of me. She herself was one of those who delight in work for work's sake, but the happiness was not sufficient unless others were working too. She used to perform prodigies in the way of 'making up' fine things, her own or someone else's, and, as she was not very strong, these excursions usually ended in a faint a-top of a hot iron. She used to make cakes with a prodigious expenditure of eggs and butter. 'For the dint of the richness,' as our old cook used to say, the cakes never would hold together, but crumbled at a touch. The crumbs were very delicious, I am bound to say.

She performed prodigies of doing, always with the maximum of discomfort to the idle. When she was in a whirlwind of doing it was an unpardonable offence for anyone else to sit down or even to lean against a wall or stand on one foot. There was a Christmas when she not only made the Christmas pudding but insisted on sitting up to see it boiled. The pudding was of such huge dimensions that there was only one pot capable of holding it. That pot was cracked. The old cook retired to bed at midnight with the caustic remark that there was no use in everybody's being worn out for Christmas Day, adding that the pudding might as well have been boiled by daylight, which was quite true. My sister was contemptuous of these unsportsmanlike remarks. To her a feast was not a feast unless it was kept strenuously. All that Christmas Eve night my sister watched the pot a-boiling, while two worn-out little girls dozed in their hard chairs. Dozed uneasily too, for the last warning of the cook had been as to the probability of the pot bursting and as like as not killing everyone of us with the splinters of iron, let alone the danger of our being scalded to death. For hours the pot threatened explosion, waking us from our uneasy slumbers. About five o'clock the pudding was considered safe, and there was only to push the pot a little to one side. My sister's behaviour to us was what that of the Wise Virgins might have been to the Foolish with their lamps out. She was quite cheerful, and she pitied us as we groped our way to bed. She had suggested going to six o'clock Mass, but that was quite beyond us.

Twenty-five Years: Reminiscences, 1913

HOME FOR CHRISTMAS

Val Mulkerns

The Christmas of that year stands out in my mind with a kind of finality. I was fourteen, and abruptly at the end of the holidays some soft, almost physical appendage of childhood seems to have fallen away, like the tail off a tadpole, and I would never be quite the same again.

My father came in a hired car to collect me from my aunt's house where I was boarded during the school term. He was ushered up in state to what they called 'the room', which was now several degrees below zero. My aunt took from his numbed hands the bright bundle of Christmas presents from Mother and fussed him into an armchair by the stark fireplace, black except for a paper fan made from newspapers which was presumably intended as a decoration. In a few freezing moments the small underpaid servant girl (recently acquired from the orphanage) came in carrying a lighted oil stove which was sometimes used in the bedrooms if anybody was sick. Those were the cold wartime years when only the poor, with tiny houses, could really keep warm. But no house I had ever known was as miserably cold as this handsome farmhouse a few miles from the marble city of Kilkenny.

'Thanks very much, Bernie,' said my father to the girl. 'And how are you this fine hearty morning?'

'Grand, sir, thanks.' When my aunt turned to get the whiskey he slipped Bernie a ten-shilling note, winking elaborately and motioning her to silence. She skipped away beaming, closing the door behind her.

'Are you sure now, Daniel, you wouldn't like the fire lit? 'Twouldn't be any trouble and indeed it would give that bone-lazy young one something to do.'

'I can't stay too long, so don't trouble yourself, Ellen.'

'Anyway,' said my aunt, 'sure the sun is so strong 'twould likely put the fire out.' She handed him his whiskey and I knew by the tight curl of his lip as he raised his glass to drink her health that he was trying to smother a laugh. Later he would tell my mother about this – Ellen's latest scientific discovery – and they would roar laughing together.

'Won't you join me, Ellen, and the festive season that's in it?'

'Sure maybe a taste of the sherry wine would be no harm and me with a cold,' my aunt agreed.

'Do you all the good in the world, Ellen,' said my father heartily, and though I could see his throat stretching for the bite of the whiskey, he waited until she had filled her glass. He was just about to give the wish when Ellen thought better of her self-indulgence and poured half of the sherry back into the bottle, spilling some in the process. She was no doubt remembering how near Christmas was, and how as many as six distant cousins might drop in over the season.

'Your good health, Ellen, and here's a happy Christmas to us all and many of them!'

'Amen to that,' said my aunt, taking a sip and then watching nervously as my father joyously swallowed half his drink in one go and smacked his lips genially after it.

'Good stuff, Ellen. The best. Warm the cockles of your heart!' and the practiced charm of his best professional smile brought a slight response even from Ellen, though you could see that a smile of any sort hurt her, as the effort to walk hurts a rheumatic.

'Tell me,' said my aunt grudgingly, 'how was it Peg couldn't have come over with you and you with the car got and all?'

'Work, Ellen, work. Christmas party dresses for gay young things who have been saving their clothes coupons which ought to have been spent on good woollen stockings to keep the cold out. All sorts of refurbished finery for the old – overcoats "turned" and that sort of thing. She said she'd have to let some of her clients down if she took the whole day off to come here. Assured me you'd understand.'

'And so I do,' Ellen conceded. 'How is she keeping, tell me?'

'Splendid form, thank God. In fact, hopelessly elevated at the thought of seeing our young friend here after three long months. I must say, Ellen, he's looking a credit to your good care. A credit.'

Head down, I continued my perusal of the mouldering fox in the glasscase, an unfailing delight because in strong winter sunlight like this you could see that really the taxidermist hadn't done such a good job. If you watched one patch of fur closely until your eyes ached, you became aware that infinitesimal life was moving along each stiffened hair, minute flaky things like the inhabitants of old damp books. No wonder. You could see the unused furniture gently steaming in the slight combined warmth of sun and oil heater. The windows of this room were always kept heremetically sealed except in high summer.

'He's a sturdy lad enough,' my aunt agreed, 'and a great help to us at the harvest.' This was dangerous talk although she was too stupid to be aware of it. My father might easily inquire why I hadn't been at school then. But my aunt's tongue, loosened by the sherry, ran on. 'Your Danny reminds me something wonderful of Martin, you know. Come over here till you look at him the year before he left the priests' college when we still thought he was going on for a priest.'

My father went at her bidding to the far wall, blotched with damp, whose mud-coloured wallpaper fell in loose folds around the smiling face of my disreputable uncle. The photographer seemed to have caught the moment before a wink. His clerical collar looked like fancy dress and if the family had looked honestly at him they'd have known themselves

159

that he had his own future planned despite them.

'Look at the chin now,' said my aunt, 'and the cock of the head and the way the hair grows over the forehead. The dead spit of Dan. Look up at us now, Danny boy.' I did, and instantly lowered my head again as my father nodded.

'You have a point there, Ellen, no doubt about it.' He had not allowed himself to be separated from his drink, and now swallowed the remainder with relish, maybe for consolation.

'I don't suppose you'd take another drop, Daniel?' said my aunt in the tone of voice that made lady visitors refuse another slice of madeira cake. . .

'You're in a great hurry,' said my aunt slyly. 'You wouldn't let me fill your glass again to keep the cold out, Daniel?'

'I wouldn't, Nellie. My insulation is completed now.' As I went to him he bent to examine the dusty artificial roses in the bowl on the table, into which little sprigs of lurid green celluloid holly had been stuck. 'There's a touch of the artist about you, Ellen,' he said, and I could have cheered at the wickedness of him. 'Before I go won't you allow me to wish a happy Christmas to my niece and nephew, Ellen? Where have you hidden them?'

'Ann and Matthew is below stairs with the young one,' my aunt said, somewhat put out. 'They have a cold on them and we didn't bother cleaning them up today.'

'Nevertheless.' His smile was really quite charming as well as indomitable, and my aunt Ellen reluctantly led the way downstairs. The fact is, he really *liked* children. In the kitchen, glowing with warmth from the unguarded fire, we found Ann wiping her nose on a dirty pinafore and Matthew throwing small pieces of torn-up paper into the fire and watching them roar up the chimney. Bernie made at once for the yard as my aunt appeared.

'I shouldn't do that, Matthew,' my father said, lifting the small boy up in one arm and Ann in the other. 'Little boys who do that have a habit of not growing up.' He smiled at both children and they beamed back with delighted grubby faces. . . Just before we left he produced, to my utter astonishment, two brown paper parcels from his pocket and I knew he must have stopped on the way to buy them himself: Mother's presents would have been with the big brightly-wrapped bundle upstairs.

We left Matthew racing a toy car around the kitchen and Ann with a small curly-haired black doll snug in her pinafore pocket. Colds and all, they rushed out into the icy farmyard to wave goodbye and I had never seen them so animated. I knew that if toys were given to them for birthdays or Christmas which were judged to be 'too good', they were often taken away by my aunt to be donated elsewhere after the children had forgotten them.

'Curious,' my father mused as we drove away, 'a study for an anthropologist, that family.' Suddenly he braked, got out of the car when we were half way down the lane, and ran back towards my waving aunt. 'Compliments of the season to P.J.' he shouted, and my aunt called genially, 'I'll tell him, Daniel. He's away out with a sick cow.' Impatiently I waited until my father returned and urged him to drive as fast as he could until that loathsome place was out of sight.

At home everything was beautiful. Even the brasses on the green hall door glittered as I'd never noticed before and a huge mass of red-berried holly was arranged in a brass pot-stand before the fresh white lace curtains. In the dark little hall there was more holly and ivy and then suddenly there was my mother rushing from her sewing-machine to scoop me up like a small boy into her arms. She smelled of *eau de cologne* and her brown hair newly-washed was breaking loose from its pins and she had apple cheeks. Not handsome, not young, but unlike her sister Ellen, wholesome and reassuring and – suddenly I saw it – happy. . .

Father attempted to heap more coal on the blazing fire, pausing to say over his shoulder to my mother: 'Are you sure now, Peg, you didn't let the sun at this fire earlier in the day? – it looks a bit dawny to me!'

And then all the news of Gurteenbeg came out, my mother laughing as she was expected to do over Ellen's theory about the sun's destructive rays. Wandering restlessly around the cosy room, I wanted to tell her about the full horrors of the place I had left, but I found it difficult.

She and my father regarded the O'Boyle marriage as something to be amused at and, certainly, to be grateful for since they couldn't afford to send me to St. John's College as a boarder. There was something slightly affectionate in their jeering which disturbed me. They didn't *know*.

Off and on during Christmas I tried to tell them. It was hopeless. I tried to tell them – especially my mother – how I hated Gurteenbeg and everybody in it except Bernie. I tried to tell her about the hunger and the cold that were part of accepted daily life there, about the gloom that settled over my head like a cloud as I approached the house from school every evening, about evil-smelling P.J. and the crimping meanness of Ellen. My mother turned the talk so neatly whenever I approached danger points that quite suddenly I realised she didn't want to know. She didn't want to know because boarding with the O'Boyles for the moderate sum agreed on was my only chance of a 'suitable' education, the sort neither she nor my father had been given, that would in due course lead to the University in Dublin and all they desired for me. My acceptance of the O'Boyle footbridge for what it was, they took for granted, and as Christmas ebbed away I began to grow desperate. . .

And so came the day when we put away the Christmas baubles in cardboard boxes, as we did every year, and the fire was noisy with dry crackling holly. That was the day I made my last appeal.

'Don't send me back and I'll do anything for you.'

'Such as?' grinned my father.

'Such as studying night and day at home for my exam even if it kills me,' I said recklessly.

'In which case you wouldn't pass it,' said my father. 'Look, Dan, you know you *have* to go to school.'

'Can't you let me go back to the Christian Brothers, then?'

'Why not?' said my father happily, always less fiercely ambitious than my mother. 'Why not, Peg?'

But this was apparently too much. Dropping a box that had once held Christmas crackers and would now house the glass baubles which she had protected with tissue paper over the years, my mother flung herself into an armchair and wept noisily as my father and I swept the shattered spun glass off the carpet. Then I helped him wrap up again in their coloured tissues those baubles which had escaped the holocaust.

We put them away on the highest shelf of the china cupboard and I knew with a shrivelling of the soul that Christmas was over and that Gurteenbeg with its multiple miseries must be faced, as my father advised, like a man. And indeed in the clear cold challenge of January I knew too that I would never under any circumstances think like a child again.

An Idle Woman, 1980

MY MOTHER'S DAY

Robert Cranny

Christmas Day was my mother's day. Is there anything like the smell in the house on Christmas morning? The turkey in the oven and the gentle cooking sound. A soft crackling. The ham and the goose done the day before. The trifles sitting on the table. Food everywhere. Cakes and puddings. My mother's face beaming, all for the joy of having it. No shortage of anything. Abundance. We were not missing a thing. A Christmas like no other after all the years of deprivation. There wasn't room for another thing. And bottles of stout, too. And a bottle of whiskey. They had come up from Goggins's in the thick dark purple bags. And the breakfast that morning. The kitchen nearly floated away. The lovely red glow of the fire, and my father with black shoe polish shining his boots. I got new football boots that year, too. Beautiful soft black leather. I couldn't stop looking at them. I placed them in the middle of the kitchen floor and stood back and looked at them. Heavenly morning. Only room for joy. I couldn't take my eyes off them even as I sat at the table. I wanted to kiss them. Paul sat at the table smiling, looking out through his red eyes, his hair over his forehead, a cup of tea sitting before him. I never wanted to leave the house.

The kitchen was so bright. There were three new ties hanging around my father's neck, and my mother paused to wipe her hands on her apron while Mary made her try on her new gloves. She was embarrassed. New gloves. How long had it been since she had had a new pair? She held her hands out in front of her and beamed at them. She arched her arms and struck a pose like the ads in the newspaper and we laughed at her. And then Mary placed a lovely green scarf around my mother's neck. It was huge and it draped over her shoulders. She looked beautiful. Green was her colour. Her hair was becoming whiter. She was like a queen who had found her palace again. My father looked at her and smiled. His eyes glistened and he sniffed and turned away. Always embarrassed at each other's joy. He had tenderness; he fought his tears. Paul looked on, too, opening and closing his eyes and batting his eyelids, all the time that mad smile on his face. Mary moved to my mother and gave her a hug, and then my mother turned away quickly and said, 'You'll all be late for Mass.'

My father was ready. He wore one of his new ties and he kept fussing with the knot and stretching his neck and moving his chin back and forth. It looked perfect to me. Finally he turned around and faced us and said, 'If you two hurry I'll walk down with you.' I ran for my coat and Paul shaved quickly and when he was ready we all left together. The three of us walked together through the snow that was piled high. The sun was shining and the brightness dazzled us. The sky was a deep blue, nearly purple, dancing before our eyes. I walked between my father and Paul. I felt safe and new. I had never been with them in that way and now we nodded and saluted everyone who passed us and my father kept saying, 'God that's a morning.' And he said, 'I've never seen your mother so happy. Did you see her with the gloves on? Oh, she's in heaven. Sure my God I've never seen her look forward to anything the way she did to this day.' Paul nodded and stared ahead. The wind was blowing softly, and we walked into it. I wanted to pull them with me and run and jump and laugh out aloud.

On us thy Poor Children, 1982

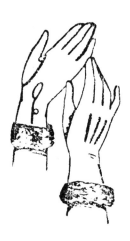

FARMER'S SON

P.J.O'Connor Duffy

There is the house with the orchard beside it,
Christmas snows deepening in front of the door,
There are the acres in which we had prided
As in the old Irish name that we bore;
Not that we spoke of the solemn deep feeling
When stirred at the heart, quickening all unto good,
But – oh, we loved them: the farm and the shieling,
The bog and the mountain, the stream and the wood!

Principle: that was my father's unspoken
Keyword to cherished and strictly-kept code,
The debt always paid and the promise unbroken,
Calm, decent, kind ways and a comely abode;
Charity, but in a sensible measure
What he scorned most were the sham and the lie –
Labour stood always the title to pleasure;
Faith was the light of his proud-gazing eye.

Proud he was – proud. And little I reckoned
Pride would cleave hearts, ending all that had been. . .
Yet desolation came. Beauty had beckoned,
Found me my true love; and she was my queen!
Then, sudden, cold, the voice of my father:
'Other and wise designs must be fulfilled,
You are my only son, but I would rather
See you a beggar than wed as you've willed!'

So,with upbraiding, grave counsel, stern warning,
Pride would belittle the love my heart sang.
She whom I visioned as fair as the morning
Would be cast down to the earth whence she sprang:
Her folk had nothing, and they were but dreamers,
She was, he vowed, no whit better than they.
(Her folk, ranked now with our country's redeemers!
She, whose white soul lit God's loveliest clay. . .!)

165

'Think, think of all that yourself will be losing –
Wed her,' said he, 'and you go from the glen!'
Vainly I pleaded, then true to my choosing,
Went from the house and came home not again. . .
My love and I prospered: she was my omen
Always of fortune, of gifts that abide –
Heaven be kind to the richest-dowered woman
Ever in poverty stood by man's side!

Now by the house with its orchard untended,
Christmas snows white by the ancient closed door,
Age broods on youth and the promise pride ended –
Pride, and the ungathered fruit that it bore!
Dust 'mid far shrines is my love and her beauty,
Dust is my father this many a year;
Time ends the conflict 'twixt duty and duty –
Her son is saying: 'Our home shall be here. . .'

An Gaedhael, Christmas 1936

CHRISTMAS COME

Patrick Macrory

Christmas was quite the most exciting moment of the Ardmore year, the time when all our hopes and joys seemed to come to a climax, and so I have kept it for the last chapter of these memories.

For me the happiness of the season became intensified when it began with the return from the preparatory school far off in County Down to which I had been sent when not yet nine years old. To come home from Mourne Grange at any time was joy but to come home for Christmas was very heaven. First, in the darkness of a winter morning, the ten-mile drive in the school bus to the railway station at Warrenpoint; the train journey up to Belfast, with everyone happy and friendly, for then no bullies strike, so hallowed and so gracious is the time. Across Belfast from the Great Northern Railway's terminus to York Street station, noting uneasily that the tram cars were caged in wire netting to fend off the bombs which in those days of the early 1920s the IRA would occasionally hurl at them. Then climbing aboard the Derry Express at York Street and off we went on the last lap of this delectable journey.

For its first few miles the train in those days skirted the northern shore of Belfast Lough, with its mudflats, groynes and seagulls, before turning inland through Antrim, Ballymena and Ballymoney, while I sat gazing entranced out of the window at the frozen fields, the bare trees white with hoar frost, the dark cold waters of the little rivers which from time to time appeared alongside the line. They all seemed to spell out the one magic word, 'Christmas!'

At Coleraine, when we had shed the part of the train that was to go directly down the branch line to Portrush, we proceeded cautiously across the Bann on a bridge that was supposed to be unsafe, down the left bank of the river, alongside the golf links where I had nursed my uneasy thoughts of death, to Castlerock, after which the train plunged into the two exciting tunnels beneath Downhill. When it emerged again into daylight the stormy winter sea was on the right, the waves crashing on to the rocks, and on the left the steep cliffs with the waterfalls cascading down their face. Then at last, as excitement grew to its climax, the train would come steaming round the bend into Limavady Junction and I would peer eagerly out of the window to see whether Mummy had brought the car to meet me there. Sometimes she had and sometimes she hadn't but it didn't really matter because in its own way the train journey from Limavady Junction to Limavady was just as exciting. And then I was *home,* and what was more, home for Christmas!

I can hardly believe that any children ever enjoyed Christmas more than we did, and for this all the credit goes unstintingly to Rosie, who was determined that it should be a memorable feast and took infinite pains to ensure that it should be so. It would have been a very different matter if it had been left to Frank, who showed himself remarkably indolent about the whole occasion. 'What do you think I should give Rosie for Christmas?' he was once heard to ask plaintively. 'Do you mean next Christmas?' asked someone for it was already past seven o'clock on the evening of Christmas Eve. 'No, no,' he said petulantly, 'I mean *this* Christmas', and no doubt ended up as usual with a modest and unimaginative cheque.

One of the secrets of Rosie's success was that we should all be involved in the preparations, beginning with the ritual stirring of the pudding back in November, though this, of course, was something I had to miss after I had been sent to boarding school. Then, a few days before Christmas, we were sent out to search the wintry wood and hedgerows for berried holly with which to decorate the hall, the drawing room and the dining room. By Christmas Eve excitement was mounting hourly. That afternoon Rosie used to sit at the long dining room table parcelling up presents for the feudal retainers in the little cottages – practical gifts of groceries, cakes, biscuits, bags of sweets striped in violent pinks and whites, bottles of grocer's port at three shillings the bottle. At six o'clock, when all had been carefully wrapped, labelled and loaded into a handcart, we were sent off to distribute them, setting off alone up the dark avenue with lanterns and torches and wearing the nearest we could get from the dressing-up box to the costumes of Dickensian waits. A selective memory tells me that in those days Christmas Eve was always fine and dry, with never a cloud in the frosty starlit night sky. At each cottage we would announce our arrival by singing carols, which I presently learnt to accompany after a fashion on a ukelele – of all inappropriate instruments! The result was pretty horrible. Dana and Hope could sing in tune but only in thin reedy tones, while Bill and Nonie, though blessed with powerful voices, were almost tone-deaf and brayed discordantly. At times the cacophony was so awful that the choir would peter out into helpless giggles while the leader, strumming madly on the ukelele, hissed at them angrily 'Sing, damn you all, sing! Oh, why can't you sing?'

Long before we reached the end of the first verse of 'Good King Wenceslas' the top of the cottage half-door would have opened to let the warm yellow light of the oil lamps stream out into the night, with our admiring audience framed in the doorway. They were not dismayed by our raucous noise and if they were eager for the carol to end it was because their chief interest lay in the distribution of presents which they knew would follow when we could be persuaded to stop singing. The hands came eagerly out, sometimes too eagerly, as on the occasion when a bottle of port slipped from old James Mullan's trembling fingers to be shattered on the stone-flagged floor and somebody had to race back to Ardmore for a replacement. By the time we had completed our round we would have walked two miles or more, hurrying nervously past the dark churchyard of Balteagh for fear of the spectres that might be abroad, for although Christmas Eve was a happy night we also knew that it was on Christmas Eve that Marley's ghost had appeared to Scrooge. Then, with the empty handcart, we trudged back to the welcoming lights of Ardmore, glowing with a mixture of exercise and a sense of conscious virtue. It was the perfect start to Christmas for there was the warming thought that our own pleasures were still to come.

I used to go to bed on Christmas Eve feeling far too excited to sleep but somehow I had always dropped off before the long black stocking was laid gently across the foot of my bed. If I woke in the small hours I could wriggle my toes to feel its weight and hear the thrilling rustle of the wrapping paper but I always observed the rule that stockings must not be opened before 6.30 am. By some inbuilt alarm system we all woke on the dot and so had come to the first item in Rosie's carefully planned programme, the opening of the stocking. She knew very well that if everything happened at once the rest of the day would be an anti-climax and had so arranged things that all through Christmas Day there would be something else to which we could look forward. Stocking-opening was the overture.

We knew very well by now that Father Christmas was really Rosie and even today, sixty years later, I am filled with admiration and gratitude when I think of the trouble that she must have taken over those stockings. She must have sat up half the night wrapping the presents and have spent half the year before that collecting them by visits to Woolworths in Derry and careful study of the mail order catalogues from Gamages and Hamleys. They were small, as befitted stocking presents, but always exciting and imaginative; conjuring tricks, cap pistols, little men whose rubber faces could be squeezed into grotesque expressions, huge tin beetles, spotted green and red, which were pulled backwards once or twice to wind up the spring and then released to crawl across the floor. I remember well 'Old Mr Electric Whiskers', the sculptured metallic face of an old man whose chin, when rubbed with a magic ring, sprouted feathery white whiskers and continued to do so until the chemical was exhausted. Always there were musical instruments and very early in the morning the house was full of music of a sort. While I tried out a new mouth organ I could hear from the bedroom which Dana and Hope shared next door the pipe of a penny whistle or the tinkle of a toy xylophone, as from Bill's distant quarters on a lower floor there came the toot of a trumpet.

After breakfast we were sent up to the nursery to wait for the drawing room to be made ready for the next event in the programme, the giving of 'the Big Presents', the gifts from Frank and Rosie, from Uncle Jock and Aunt Irene in distant India and from taciturn Aunt Agnes, the permanent paying guest. While we waited we passed the time in gloatingly showing each other what we had got in our presents, nor can I ever remember any jealousy on that score. Then the gong sounded far away in the hall and a thundering herd cascaded down the nursery stairs and charged into the drawing room, sniffing round eagerly like hounds at check until each had found the chair piled high with the presents that bore his or her name. So far as presents were concerned this was the highlight of the day, although there would be more to come in the evening. Invariably my presents were, in that time-honoured but not always completely truthful phrase, 'exactly what I wanted', although I can remember few of them today. But I have never forgotten my first train set, a Bassett-Lowke Gauge O. I had been invited to choose its components from Gamages' catalogue and had modestly selected one of the cheaper engines, costing £1, but what I got was a magnificent King George V class express engine which I had coveted but had not dared to suggest, since it cost all of 42/-. The carriages were in the chocolate and yellow livery of the old London and North-Western Railway, which shows you how long ago it was.

The presents from Aunt Agnes were awaited with special interest because, gruff though she might be, she had plenty of money, she was generous and her gifts were imaginative. It is possible that she supplied the generosity and Rosie the imagination. Sometimes she gave us a joint present, such as an oil-fired cooking stove with three burners and an oven, on which we could practise cookery in the nursery (although our efforts seldom got beyond making toffee on a wet afternoon). On another occasion she gave us a wooden switchback railway which we erected on the lawn, taking it in turns to climb the ladder to the platform and then come coasting down on the little rubber-wheeled trolley. Later we used to take this contraption to village fetes and church bazaars and it proved to be a real money-spinner at a penny a ride.

Days that are Gone, 1983

HOMING SONG AT CHRISTMAS

I

Now in the Christmas gloaming
And to the lighted hearth
The absent ones come homing
From all the ends of earth.

II

Come in, dear hearts and rest
Ere this good hour be flown,
Hand to hand, breast to breast
Beloveds every one.

III

Ere the good time be over,
Come stepping warm and light
Friend to friend, lover to lover,
Welcomed in from the night:

Katharine Tynan.

ACKNOWLEDGEMENTS

Grateful acknowledgement is made to:

Gerald Annesley for permission to quote from *As the Sight is Bent* by Lady Mabel Annesley;

Appletree Press for permission to quote from *The Humour is on Me* by Eamon Kelly;

Batsford Ltd for permission to quote from *In Kerry Long Ago* by John O'Donoghue;

Sam Hanna Bell for permission to quote from *Erin's Orange Lily*;

Simon Campbell for permission to reprint 'The star' by Joseph Campbell;

The Estate of Padraic Colum for permission to reprint 'Rake down the fire';

Curtis Brown Ltd for permission to quote from *Letters of C.S. Lewis*;

Century Hutchinson Ltd for permission to quote from *Light a Penny Candle* by Maeve Binchy and from *The Mountain Man* by Tim Daly;

J.M. Dent & Sons Ltd for permission to reproduce illustrations by Robert Gibbings;

André Deutsch Ltd and A.P. Watt Ltd for permission to quote from *The Emperor of Ice Cream* by Brian Moore;

Bobby Devlin for permission to quote from *An Interlude with Seagulls*;

Norman Dugdale for permission to reprint 'Home for Christmas';

Dundalgan Press Ltd for permission to quote from *At Slieve Gullion's Foot* by Michael J. Murphy;

Faber and Faber Ltd for permission to reprint 'Turkeys observed' from *Death of a Naturalist* by Seamus Heaney, and 'An eclogue for Christmas' by Louis MacNeice from *Selected Poems*, to quote from *The Barracks* by John McGahern and to reproduce an illustration;

Fr Denis Faul and Fr Raymond Murray for permission to reproduce an illustration;

Allen Figgis & Co. Ltd for permission to quote from *The Way that I Went* by Robert Lloyd Praeger;

Rowel Friers for permission to reproduce an illustration;

The Gallery Press for permission to quote from *Two for a Woman, Three for a Man* by Michael Coady, and from *A Drink of Spring* by John Ennis;

Gill and Macmillan Ltd for permission to quote from *In Great Haste: The Letters of Michael Collins and Kitty Kiernan*, edited by Leon O Broin;

The Goldsmith Press Ltd for permission to quote from *The Complete Poems of Patrick Kavanagh*, published by The Goldsmith Press, Newbridge, Co. Kildare;

John Hewitt for permission to reprint 'Christmas Eve';

Paul Hogarth for permission to reproduce an illustration;

The Irish Manuscripts Commission for permission to quote from *The Correspondence of Daniel O'Connell*;

The *Irish Times* for permission to reprint 'Santa Claus needs a helping hand' from *Man Bites Dog* by Donal Foley;

Peggy Kelly for permission to reproduce an illustration;

Michael Longley, Salamander Press and Gallery Press for permission to reprint 'The goose' from *Poems 1963–1983*;

Macmillan, London and Basingstoke for permission to quote from *Brendan Behan: Interviews and Recollections, volume 2*, by Beatrice Behan;

Macmillan, London and Basingstoke, and Holt Rinehart & Winston for permission to quote from *The Year of the French* by Thomas Flanagan;

Macmillan Publishing Co. (N.Y.) for permission to quote from *The Letters of Sean O'Casey, volume 1, 1910–41*, edited by David Krause (copyright © 1975 by Macmillan Publishing Co.);

Marshall, Morgan & Scott Publications Ltd for permission to quote from *A Road Too Wide* by David Armstrong with Hilary Saunders;

The Mercier Press for permission to quote from *Stories from a Kerry Fireside* by J.B. Keane;

Methuen London Ltd for permission to quote from *Put Money in thy Purse* by Micheál Mac Liammóir;

Muller, Blond & White Ltd for permission to quote from *My Life and Easy Times* by Patrick Campbell;

John Murray Ltd for permission to reprint 'The crib in the Carmelite Church, Dublin' from *Songs from Leinster* by W.M. Letts;

The National Museum of Ireland for permission to quote from *Christmas and the Children* by Anne O'Dowd and Mairead Reynolds;

North-West Books for permission to quote from *Days that are Gone* by Patrick Macrory;

Michael O'Beirne for permission to quote from *Mister: A Dublin Childhood*;

O'Brien Press for permission to quote from *Your Dinner's Poured Out* by Paddy Crosbie, and from *Jimeen* by Padraig Ó Siochfhradha;

A.D. Peters & Co. Ltd for permission to quote from *An Only Child* by Frank O'Connor, and from *Lovers of their Time and other Stories* by William Trevor;

Poolbeg Press for permission to quote from *Wilson Place* by Brendan O'Byrne, and from *An Idle Woman* by Val Mulkerns;

The Public Record Office of Northern Ireland for permission to quote from *The Drennan Letters* by Dr Wm Drennan;

Martin Secker & Warburg Ltd for permission to quote from *Down All the Days* by Christy Brown;

The Society of Authors on behalf of the Bernard Shaw Estate for permission to quote from *Music in London 1890–94* by George Bernard Shaw;

The Society of Authors as the literary representative of the Estate of James Joyce, Jonathan Cape Ltd and the Viking Press for permission to quote from *The Dead* by James Joyce;

Abner Stein and Stein & Day Inc. (N.Y.) for permission to quote from *On us thy Poor Children* by Robert Cranny;

Talbot Press Ltd for permission to quote from *Peig* by Peig Sayers (translated into English by Bryan MacMahon), and from *Joking Apart* by J.D. Sheridan; and to reproduce an illustration by Paul Noonan;

Anne Yeats and Michael B. Yeats, owners of the copyright of Jack B. Yeats, for permission to reproduce illustrations originally published by the Cuala Press;

Michael B. Yeats for permission to reprint 'The second coming' by W.B. Yeats.

The publishers have made every effort to trace and acknowledge copyright holders. We apologise for any omissions in the above list and we will welcome additions or amendments to it for inclusion in any reprint edition.

INDEX OF AUTHORS